Windshifts

A True Story of Adventure And Triumph Over Breast Cancer

Jane Grossman

authorHOUSE™

1663 LIBERTY DRIVE, SUITE 200
BLOOMINGTON, INDIANA 47403
(800) 839-8640
WWW.AUTHORHOUSE.COM

First published by AuthorHouse 08/11/05

ISBN: 1-4208-3759-1 (sc)
ISBN: 1-4208-6982-5 (dj)

Printed in the United States of America
Bloomington, Indiana

This book is printed on acid-free paper.

This book is dedicated with love to

Ken

my husband and soul mate.

Path of Grace

"A woman's path need not always take her many miles from home. It will, however, always invite her to let go of where she's already been, and to be open to the mystery of where she's going. Grace will be her guide and will ask her to trust in her own wisdom. In this way, a woman's path will invariably lead her back to her true self, and no path is ever more valuable than this."

Sally Lowe Whitehead

Iniki - A 34 foot Pacific Seacraft Crealock

Chapter 1
The Wind Reversal

The wind shifted. I sat in the cockpit of our sailboat with a cup of coffee and barely noticed. My view changed slightly as the boat swung 45 degrees with the gentle breeze, but I thought nothing of it. The shift was too subtle to alert me to impending danger.

I lived aboard *Iniki*, our 34 ft. sloop, with my husband, Ken. At that time we were moored in Bonaire, one of the "ABC" Islands in the Caribbean Sea. Safely south of the hurricane zone, Aruba, Bonaire and Curacao lay 80 miles off the coast of Venezuela.

From my cushion in the cockpit I gazed off our stern. A second row of sailboats flying flags from around the world bobbed gently on the calm, clear water. Less than 2000 meters beyond them, tall cactus caught the first sunrays of the new day on Klein Bonaire, a tiny, undeveloped island next to Bonaire. A flock of loras, indigenous green parrots, flew toward the small island. Their incessant squawking in flight disrupted the stillness of the morning.

Every morning the same old man sat in his little rowboat and fished *his* spot. Hunched over the side, his dark-skinned face lost in the shadow of his floppy straw hat, he jerked the hand line. Hand over hand, he pulled up the monofilament while three sea gulls circled above him, looking for an easy meal. The hook came up empty. The fisherman put on more bait and tossed out the line again.

Most mornings I had about an hour of peace and serenity to write in my journal or just meditate on nature before the irritating static noise of our single sideband radio interrupted my thoughts. Once tuned into the NOAA weather channel, Ken diligently took notes from the weird, monotone computer voice that repeated the weather conditions for our corner of the Caribbean.

The grating radio noise never bothered Ken. *Why is that? He complains if I just turn on a hair dryer!* Ken was good at tuning in frequencies and could get broadcasts from all around the world, which was how we got our news. He even kept a weather notebook and updated forecasts two or three times a day to see the weather patterns and how they develop. Our life aboard *Iniki* revolved around the weather. Highs, lows and stationary fronts punctuated our cruising plans. The weather dictated when to go, when to stay, when to seek shelter and put out a second anchor.

That Tuesday morning, October 28, 1998, there was no radio static to annoy me. Ken left on a business trip to Caracas, Venezuela, the previous day and would be away from the island for six days. The two of us had lived aboard our sailboat for over two years. In the past, anytime I stayed on the boat alone we first brought it into a slip in a marina for safety and security reasons. Bonaire had two first class marinas. Both offered great protection from seas and winds that made them stifling hot and buggy. So I didn't want to stay there.

"I'll be perfectly fine by myself out on the mooring while you're gone," I assured Ken, presenting my case. "It's not a big deal. I'll be much cooler out in the breeze, plus I'll be closer to town."

Bonaire is a desert island with a thriving coral reef circling most of it only a short distance from shore. On the western lee side of Bonaire, between the living reef and the shoreline, lies a shelf of old dead coral covered with a thin layer of sand. That made for very tenuous holding for boats wanting to anchor off the charming Dutch island.

A member of the royal family of The Netherlands had donated a substantial sum of money to install a mooring system on Bonaire. Mooring cans attached to huge, submerged concrete blocks provide safe, secure holding for the visiting cruising boats and protect the coral from anchor damage. In normal conditions the eastern trade winds cause the moored sailboats to face land with their bows into the wind. The ocean floor drops so quickly that a moored boat's bow could be in 15 feet of water while the stern hangs over the edge of the reef in 200 feet of water.

Ken and I took great delight in the underwater wonderland right under our hull. No scuba tanks required. I regularly saw interesting marine life: schools of Blue Tang swimming in unison; a brilliant Rainbow Parrot Fish hovering in a "fish cleaning station" while small "cleaning fish" darted in and out of its gills and mouth unharmed; a flat flounder lying motionless on the bottom, perfectly camouflaged in the sand; an eel slithering out of a coral head and into the hole of another; a pair of spotted eagle rays "flying" by, disappearing into the deep blue.

In the cockpit, sipping my second cup of coffee, I thought about the day ahead. I was excited about having a few days to myself. Let's face it--cozy togetherness with the one you love is dandy, but a bit of breathing room every once in a while can be a good thing. I looked forward to doing whatever I wanted to do, whenever I wanted to do it. I figured I would get the work projects on my "To Do" list out of the way; then I could goof off with a clear conscience.

"Teak" was the word for the day. *Iniki* was a Pacific Seacraft Crealock, a beautiful blue water cruiser with a dark green hull, brass fittings and teak trim. The tropical sun and salt water are brutal on the varnished bright work and she needed a touch-up. The weather report from the night before predicted a clear day with no rain--just what I needed to get the job done. There was, however, mention of a tropical storm named Mitch located north and west of Bonaire. Even though Mitch was increasing in strength and was predicted to become a hurricane, it moved further away from Bonaire.

So tropical storm Mitch was not a concern for me....I thought.

I got busy and cleaned, taped and lightly sanded all the exterior teak. Then I applied two coats of varnish. In between coats I reorganized the cabinets and lockers below. That was a much easier task without bumping into another person every time I turned around.

There was actually a surprising amount of storage space on board *Iniki*. We had removed the cushion from the aft berth and used that area to store spare parts, dive gear, spear guns and miscellaneous stuff. Compartments under the

V-berth and each of the settees in the salon provided more storage. Still, space on the boat was at a premium and had to be used efficiently.

Regardless of what had to be retrieved, it always seemed to turn into an archeological dig to find the desired item and often turned up surprises long forgotten. Generally, I knew where everything was. Under the starboard settee, pasta, tuna fish, diced tomatoes, salsa and oil were neatly packed in plastic containers next to a spare danforth anchor and chain, spare alternator and large black tool bag. Rice, flour, pancake mix, condiments, snacks, canned vegetables, canned fruit, dried beans and lentils were under the port settee.

I took an inventory of provisions on hand. We still had large containers full of lentils that we bought before we left the States. *Why on earth did we lug around 25 pounds of lentils for the past two years? What were we thinking?* I didn't know what to expect when we started out. It had been a learning experience to discover what worked well on a boat and what didn't. We proved that lentils keep well for long periods of time but we were never so remote or low on food that I wanted to steam up an already-hot environment with a nice big pot of lentil soup. I tossed the lentils overboard that day. Let the fish enjoy them!

After a long day's work I was absorbed in a good book that kept me up reading later than usual. It was nearly midnight when I climbed into the V-berth, ready to sleep. Before I could get comfortable I felt a change in the boat's movement. Waves slapped the hull. The wind whistled through the rigging. *Something is wrong!* Alarmed, I got back up to have a look around outside.

Standing by the companionway I noticed that the winds shifted and swiftly increased from zero to twenty knots as it clocked around from east to south to west. The driving rain came next. Lightning illuminated the clouds to the west. The sky rumbled.

"Oh no!" I groaned out loud to myself. "Please don't let this be happening!"

My biggest fear while I was alone on a mooring was a wind reversal. Mitch, the named storm soon to become one of the deadliest hurricanes of the century, had influenced the weather in the Southeastern Caribbean and caused an interruption of the normal eastern trade winds. A wind reversal was in progress.

Wind reversals happen in Bonaire only a couple of times a year. Boats on moorings swing around 180 degrees, which places them treacherously close to the rocky shore. But the real danger comes with the large swells and breaking waves. Their force can snap mooring lines, rip out cleats and toss the boats up on the rocks.

The harbormaster of Bonaire is on constant watch for wind reversals and there's usually several hours notice to mariners. Warnings of potential danger are broadcast on television. Radio stations announce wind reversal alerts on the air. When forewarned and prepared the local fishing boats, dive boats, tour boats and recreational boats could take shelter in the marina or go out to sea until the crisis was over.

We did not have a T.V. on board and I did not listen to the local radio stations that night. Out on deck in the wind and rain, I was suddenly very wide-awake.

Strong gusts strained the flapping awning, so I hauled it down and cleared the excess stuff out of the cockpit area. The rain didn't last long and the wind soon dropped back down to dead calm.

Maybe the worst is over. I hoped it was true but I didn't quite believe it. I sat up a while to watch the wind and seas. Just then the big swells began to roll in from the west. Like a giant pendulum, *Iniki* rocked so much from side to side that it felt like her mast would hit the water.

Down below, the coffee pot crashed on the floor. Books flew off the shelves. Pans and dishes banged and clanged. I stuffed towels everywhere to stop the racket. Since there was no wind to hold all the moored boats in the same direction, they were rolling and swinging every which way, masts and sterns too close for comfort. *Iniki's* stern was nearly on top of the building breaking waves.

I looked around and saw flashlights on boats nearby. Other cruisers were also up and alert to the situation. I watched as a few left the mooring area to ride it out at sea, while other boats in deeper water on the outside moorings stayed put.

On shore it was the eve of a local holiday--Antillean Day. I could hear the loud music blasting from the huge speakers at Karel's Tiki Bar, full of dancing partiers. The festive mood seemed odd and inappropriate considering the danger and drama I faced on the water. The pleasure of my solitude was gone and I longed for Ken's experience, skill and strength. I needed his gift of clear, quick thinking in emergency situations.

My mind raced. *What should I do? Should I stay and ride it out? Should I call someone for help? Who?* I figured everyone I knew would be busy dealing with this. *Should I take the boat off the mooring? What if I screw up and end up on the rocks?*

I had handled the boat plenty of times before but there was always someone else on board. I had *never* single-handed her before. I remembered that Ken had said in case of a wind reversal we would simply slip off the mooring lines and go sailing for a while. *Slipping the lines was simple with two people, but could I do it by myself with these big rollers pushing me around?*

The sound of my pounding heart seemed to amplify in my head. I wanted to shut my eyes and have the nightmare go away. *Maybe I'll be all right if I just sit tight.* But I could not shake the thoughts that kept creeping back into my mind: *Land is danger! Get away from the shore! It is safer in deep water.*

I turned on the engine and looked for an escape route through the swinging row of boats between the open water and me. It was 2:00AM. I glanced around and mentally went over a plan of what I had to do. *Just take one step at a time.* I turned on the running lights and looked around some more. *Can I do this?* Still, I hesitated. I didn't want to risk it. I sat frozen with fear until I heard a loud crack. Startled, I looked toward the small fisherman's pier that was about two boat lengths away from me. An unattended ferryboat ripped away from the dock as I watched. The violent waves spun the boat around and bashed it up on the rocky shore. Each wave that pounded it produced a sickening sound of splintering, crunching wood. Somewhere inside its cabin a bell clanged like a death toll.

That's it! I have to go. If I stay another minute it might be our home that gets destroyed. I can do this. I MUST do this! NOW!

Spurred into action, I went forward, slipped the starboard mooring line at the bow, then went back to the wheel to keep the boat facing out to sea toward the waves. I put on the autopilot, thinking it would keep the boat straight. Timing was critical. Watching and waiting for a lull between series of waves, I hurried back to the bow to slip the port bow line and made sure all the lines were in the boat. The last thing I needed was a line wrapped around the propeller crippling the engine. That most certainly would spell disaster. Another big breaking wave pushed the boat broadside to the seas and even closer to both the shore and the sailboat next to me. Grabbing a handrail for balance, I rushed back to take the wheel.

OK, get me out of this mess! I turned the wheel and revved the engine but the boat wouldn't turn. I had no control! My mind could not grasp the problem. All I could see was the depth gauge registering less and less water under the keel as *Iniki* continued to drift towards the rocks.

What's wrong? Why is this happening? Think!

The moment seemed like an eternity before I realized that I forgot to turn off the autopilot. *Idiot!* Switching it off I turned the wheel hard over to port and gunned the engine, in forward, reverse, then forward again. *Iniki* responded and her bow came around just in time to avoid a collision with my neighbor. I plowed through the waves, then around an outside boat that was also leaving. The pulse in my head was deafening.

As I maneuvered out to deep water away from the treacherous mooring I talked out loud to myself, hoping that the sound of my own voice would keep me focused and thinking clearly. "Jane, you're OK....Take a deep breath and calm down. You're doing good...the boat is OK. Everything is going to be OK. You can do this. Keep it up!"

I swallowed my panic and reassessed my situation. It was a black night with no moon. I had another four hours until daylight. *An eternity!* In the dark everything is distorted and strange. The familiar coastline of Bonaire became hard to read in the blur of shore lights. Distances were deceptive. Ten or more other sailboats also motored around so I had to pay attention to their navigation lights to keep clear of them.

Another concern was Klein Bonaire. The flat little island was invisible in the dark with no lights. At night its surrounding reef was impossible to see. "What if..." thoughts threatening to undo me as I motored back and forth until dawn.

What if I run out of fuel? What if the high winds and squalls return? How can I leave the helm to use the head with all these boats going in circles? Can I keep this up all night? What if I can't stay awake? How did I get myself in this situation?

I looked at my watch. *Did it stop? Surely more than a minute had passed since I last looked.* No, I saw that the hand still ticked off the seconds. The night seemed endless. To pass the time and avoid scary thoughts, I sang every song I could think of and tried to remember every anchorage and town we ever visited with our boat.

And I prayed.

Relief and joy swept over me when morning finally arrived. The sun came up in a glorious display of color, chasing away the goblins of darkness and the long, stressful night. The sea was as smooth as glass. Everything appeared calm, but not quite normal. One of the other sailboats got too close to Klein Bonaire during the night and was aground on the reef at the northeast corner.

I, too, still had a dilemma. *I survived the night but what do I do with Iniki now? Maybe I could pick up the mooring again. That has to be easier than getting off last night!* So, very, very slowly, I approached the same mooring I had left hours earlier. I put the boat in neutral and she continued to glide toward my target. On the bow I leaned over the rail with boat hook in hand, but could not quite reach the line I needed to grab. I was so close! Returning to the helm, I circled the boat around for a second attempt. I leaned out over the rail again, stretching….steady…. *Yes!*

I did it! I retrieved the mooring lines and hooked them on the forward bow cleats. *Iniki* was safe and secure again. A euphoric feeling bubbled up inside me. I wanted to scream and shout! I was so proud of myself.

Then I noticed the crashed ferry boat nearby on shore. A crowd gathered around to inspect the large, jagged hole in the side of the hull. My emotions were all over the place. I felt relieved and elated, yet nervous and fearful. I was exhausted from being up all night but my adrenaline was still pumping. I went below and started to shake. Images of my struggle to save the boat and the sounds of the ferry breaking up played over and over in my head.

I sat down on the settee in the salon. Tears quickly turned to sobs. I wept with fear over my vulnerability and what could have happened to the boat and to me. All night long I fought to control my emotions in order to focus on what had to be done. I had no one else to lean on during the ordeal and had to dig down deep inside to find strength to get through the night. Now that the crisis was over it was safe to let go and release all the tensions pent up inside for so many hours.

Over the next few days Mitch spun itself into one of the most destructive hurricanes in history, killing over 18,000 people in Central America and the western Caribbean. My troubles seemed insignificant in comparison, but my thoughts about myself were altered forever. I possessed a new level of confidence. I didn't realize at the time that I would need to draw strength and courage from the experience ten months later, when I faced another crisis.

For the moment, however, I felt only post-traumatic stress. The tears and shaking finally stopped but sleep was elusive. Every time I closed my eyes fears and visions of doom rushed back into my mind. I looked around the inside of *Iniki* remembering when we bought her and thought about how far we had traveled.

Chapter 2
The Beginning

"Are you crazy?" I asked when I first heard my husband's plan. "Do you really expect me to sell everything and live on a small boat? You're not serious.... are you?"

Ken and I had been married for nearly ten years. We lived in a 108-year-old Victorian home in a western suburb of Chicago with two teenagers daughters, a large Newfoundland dog and years worth of accumulated stuff. My husband's dream was to sell our house and sail from Chicago to Venezuela. I loved to travel but the thought of giving up everything was frightening. I wanted a place to return to--a small house, a condo, apartment....something to call "home". I loved gardening, running, cross-country skiing and horseback riding. Living on a sailboat was not conducive to any of these things.

"What about holidays and visits from the kids and the rest of the family?" I demanded.

"We'll go visit the kids where they live," Ken countered, "or they can come to our boat."

I was not jumping at this idea. *Oh, having a sailboat would be fun, but there is no way I want to LIVE on one indefinitely.*

Home inside Hinsdale, Illinois

We named our boat "Iniki"--a Hawaiian word meaning "power of the wind". Ken envisioned the power of the wind carrying us to faraway lands around the world. I ignored the vision but I liked the sound of the word.

Iniki was built in Fullerton, California and was delivered to us in Chicago, brand spanking new, in August of 1993. I learned how to sail that July in preparation for her arrival. My husband had been sailing long before I met him. For the sake of our relationship, I thought it wise for me to learn to sail from someone else.

I learned the basics on a 22-foot J-boat, with a wonderful, enthusiastic teacher, and progressed at a comfortable pace. Dan, a regional racing champion with J-22s, taught me the points of sail, sailing terminology, man-overboard techniques, reefing the mainsail, tacking and jibing. *Hey, I'm pretty good at this.*

What a blast! Gliding over the water with my right hand on the tiller and my left hand on the main sheet I became part of the boat and harnessed the wind. I had often felt the same merging feeling when I rode horseback, moving with and becoming part of the horse. Sailing was equally thrilling. *But I still don't want to live on a sailboat.*

During the next two summers we sailed *Iniki* on Lake Michigan whenever possible. At the time, our business was stressful and our teenagers were rebellious and challenging. Out on the water our tension evaporated and vanished with the wind. When we passed the sea wall of Monroe Harbor, raised the sails and shut off the engine, Ken and I let out simultaneous sighs of contentment. In those peaceful moments, the idea of spending more time on the boat and leaving the long, cold Midwestern winters behind did start to sound inviting, I admitted.

I didn't mind selling our current house. It was too big. I even liked the idea of simplicity, of an uncomplicated life, if such a thing is possible. The difficult part for me was getting rid of things. I didn't want to be wasteful. *Won't we need some of these things in the future?* I assumed if we did this sailing thing we would eventually return to life as we knew it before leaving. Wrong! We would never be the same again.

I desperately wanted to cling to the known and familiar. Ken and I argued over what to keep, what to donate, what to sell. Our negotiations went room by room through the house. My protest, "But I *love* that." wasn't a good enough reason for Ken to justify paying to save and store it. He was ruthless in his goal to simplify our lives. However, a few things I insisted on keeping, rational or not. My oak drafting table, for one, was unique and the artist in me would not sacrifice it. *When we are done sailing I will still want to draw,* I told myself. Looking back I can see that letting go of everything was too drastic for me to handle. An unknown future that I could hardly imagine was a bit frightening. *Who would I be without those things? Did I have any say in the direction of my life? Of course, I could live without the drafting table, but....*

My inner struggle and resistance to such a radical change continued. Other things still worried me. *What if I don't like living aboard a boat once we're out there? Where will we end up? Are we deserting the kids? Our youngest daughter would be off to college but how would she handle our leaving Chicago? Were we being selfish and irresponsible? And how would I handle leaving my family and friends?*

I wasn't a risk taker. I generally opted for "safe" in my approach to life. Ken's attention and concern focused on boat performance and maintenance-- how many spare parts to carry, how many months worth of provisions should be stored and which charts and guidebooks to buy. Before we departed Ken earned his U.S. Coast Guard Captain's License-100 Ton Master. His knowledge and seamanship partially eased my worries about safety and security on board *Iniki*.

Maybe I was a pushover or perhaps I was brainwashed since Ken is, in fact, an expert at hypnotism, and holds a Doctorate in Clinical Hypnotherapy. Whatever the reason, the idea of cruising slowly grew on me, especially after I read about the tropical islands we would visit in the Caribbean. Photos of sun-drenched beaches lined with palm trees enticed me even more.

Eventually, I let go of my reservations and took a leap of faith to follow Ken on his dream adventure. Let the future take care of itself, I decided boldly. After all, this was a rare opportunity to go off on an incredible journey while we were able, physically and financially.

June 1996

As our departure date approached I sewed a prom dress for our daughter, Kassie, during the whirlwind of her year-end senior activities. After her graduation she found a summer job and lived with Ken's parents until college started in August. Ken and I moved aboard *Iniki* after some final preparations. We set up a mail-forwarding service, updated our wills, and visited the doctor and dentist. We both got shots for tetanus, yellow fever and hepatitis A, and I had a mammogram. As if I didn't have enough on my mind, the mammogram revealed a lump in my left breast. A biopsy was recommended.

"It looks innocent but knowing your plans to leave the country I think it's wise to remove it so we know for sure." my doctor advised.

I agreed. Less than a week before our D-Day I was scheduled for outpatient surgery. Fortunately, the extracted mass proved to be benign. With that obstacle eliminated I was ready as I would ever be....physically and mentally.... to sail off into the sunset.

July 4, 1996- Independence Day

I stood on the deck of *Iniki*, released the mooring lines and cast off from the dock of Columbia Yacht Club in Chicago. Captain Ken was at the helm. Tears ran down my face as air horns bid us adieu and friends cheered us on, offering last minute bits of advice: "Reef the main as soon as you think about it!" "Don't sail where the birds walk."

When will I see you again? We made a final pass by Chicago's beautiful waterfront, where thousands of people were enjoying the holiday and sunshine. Buckingham Fountain sprayed water skyward, saluting our departure from Monroe Harbor. Ken and I were filled with emotion and a sense of wonder about what lay ahead.

Iniki at Colunbia Yacth Club, Chicago

Heading north we day-sailed to Milwaukee then made an overnight trip to Sturgeon Bay, Wisconsin, at the base of Door County. In Sturgeon Bay we checked in on friends in town while our Cozy Cabin heater was repaired at Palmer Johnson's Marina. When we left the marina, we motored west through the Channel toward Green Bay and the leeward side of Wisconsin's Door County Peninsula. In the middle of the channel the engine alarm sounded and a red warning light flashed. Ken immediately killed the engine.

"What happened?" I asked anxiously. "We're only in Wisconsin! What could be wrong already?"

"For some reason the engine overheated. Pull out the jib and keep us in the center of the channel." Ken ordered as he disappeared below to look for the problem.

I sailed toward the bay worrying about our dilemma. I knew nothing about diesel engines. By the time I left the channel Ken figured out that a mess of seaweed was sucked up, causing the diesel engine to overheat and burn out the impeller. While we rocked and rolled in four-foot waves on Green Bay, Ken removed the alternator to get to the impeller, installed a new impeller, and then replaced the alternator. My stomach felt queasy, more from worry than the motion. Next, Ken jumped in the water to extricate the weeds from the intake. Back aboard the boat and dripping in the cockpit he reached for the ignition key and said, "Cross your fingers." The engine belched a cloud of smoke. Not good. He hit the kill switch again.

Daylight slipped away, adding to my uneasiness. We needed to get to the nearest harbor to anchor before dark. My husband informed me that we had to anchor under sail and proceeded to explain how we would go about it as we approached Egg Harbor in twenty knots of wind. *Great! Our very first night at anchor and we have problems.*

Seeing the anxiety in my eyes Ken smiled and said with excitement, "Don't worry. This will be cool!"

Sure. I took the helm and called out water depths to Ken, who was on the bow, readying the anchor. Luckily, we had lots of room to maneuver in the cove. When we got into position, on Ken's signal, I turned *Iniki* into the wind and the boat stopped. I luffed the sail and Ken let out the anchor as we drifted backward to set it. With teamwork, the plan worked perfectly.

"And that's how *real* sailors do it!" my hero proudly proclaimed.

I was impressed. "Good job, Ken but let's not do that every night."

We squared away the boat and retreated below to escape the horde of buzzing mosquitoes that descended on us at dusk. In the morning Ken jumped in the water and, with the help of a long grabber tool, pulled more gobs of seaweed out of our through-hull intake. That did the trick and we were up and running again. The captain/engineer/mechanic was beaming with the satisfaction of being able to solve the problem himself. Sailors must be self sufficient.

We proceeded to harbor hop up the peninsula to Washington Island and over to Beaver Island. From Beaver Island to Mackinaw City we raced downwind away from some spooky black thunderheads in five-foot waves. Passing under the Mackinac Bridge, *Iniki* sailed into Lake Huron toward the islands of the North Channel.

July 19, 1996

During a vigorous sail from Bois Blanc Island to Harbor Island, Ken reached for his hat lying under the dodger next to the companionway. Something moved and startled him. He let out a yell as he leaped backward banging into the binnacle. A small, bright green tree frog had been quite cozy under Ken's hat until it was disturbed. How in the world did that get there?! That little frog stayed in one spot all day. At night it moved around the deck, eating bugs I presume. Every morning for several days I searched for the frog's latest hiding spot. "Ken, guess where I found the little guy this morning?!"

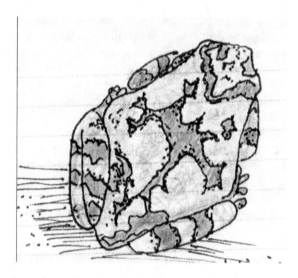

One evening, after a light rain shower, our previously silent passenger started to chirp like crazy. It was loud! Following the sound I found it sitting under the helmsman's seat with its throat all bulged out like a bubble when it croaked. That was the last night we saw Froggy. He disappeared as mysteriously as he had arrived. Maybe he answered a love call from shore and jumped ship!

July 21, 1996

To check into Canada we simply called Customs on the phone from Blind River, Ontario. Each day in the North Channel our surroundings got more wild and beautiful. Soft moss and orange lichens cushioned the rocky islands. Evergreens filled the air with the smell of Christmas. I picked bags full of sweet, wild blueberries which we ate over cereal and in pancakes. Loons, beaver and otters swam in the surrounding waters. Osprey and Eagles soared overhead, occasionally diving with talons outstretched to pluck a wiggling fish out of the water. My parched soul was awakening as I drank in the sights, sounds and smells of Nature.

In the Benjamin Islands we stopped to explore the waterfront town of Kagawong. A cute, little Anglican Church at the water's edge caught my eye. I felt drawn to it and went to look inside. The pulpit was a bow from a wooden boat. An old anchor, a wooden ship's wheel and a couple round lifesaver rings hung on the walls. At the end of each pew was a net floater on a rope. It was charming. What a welcoming sanctuary for the area watermen and their families.

August 2, 1996

One of my favorite places in the North Channel was Baie Fine, a long, narrow strip of water between two high, rocky peninsulas. McGregor's Point and Frazer Point marked the entrance on opposite sides of the band of water. We found a perfect spot in a little cove to drop our hook where there was room for only one boat next to the steep rock wall. We left *Iniki* and motored by dinghy the rest of the way to where Baie Fine opened up into an anchorage called "The Pool", which was crowded with sailboats. After we tied our dinghy to a tree, we climbed ashore and followed some hiking trails that we wanted to investigate. One led to Artist's Lake, an inspiration to many an artist, I'm sure. Colorful wildflowers encircled a pristine lake that reflected the surrounding quartz mountains.

"The only thing missing is a moose grazing knee deep in the water lilies." I said, scanning the shoreline. *I really want to see a moose.*

A second trail led us into a deep, dark fairy-tale forest within Killarney Provincial Park. The trail became steep and difficult. My flip-flops were clearly the wrong footwear for rocky mountain hiking. But the guidebook promised a spectacular view, so we trudged onward. I was thinking about sitting down for a rest when the trail opened up and abruptly ended. We stepped out on a solid, wide stone ledge and looked down. Below us, about a thousand feet or so, the surface of a brilliant mountain lake sparkled. The contrast of the surrounding white quartz peaks, highlighted with the afternoon sun, intensified the cool, rich color of the teal water.

"Wow", was all I could think of to say to no one in particular as I took in the magnificent scene. The sharp cry of a bald eagle pierced the air and echoed off the cliffs. Searching, my eyes found the large bird as it landed on a bare branch at the top of an evergreen on the far side of the lake. Looking north I could also see the sailboats clustered in the Pool below where we began our hike. It seemed like a long way away. We enjoyed the top-of-the-world perspective until dark clouds rolled in and urged us back to *Iniki*. The sky opened up as we motored back down the channel at top speed in our dinghy, trying to beat the rain. We were soaked by the time we reached *Iniki* but relieved that I had remembered to close all the hatches on the boat before we left it earlier.

Dreamer's Rock

Hole-in-the-Wall

Jane at the helm

Dewey Island, North Channel

A full month passed after leaving Chicago before I finally started to unwind and really relax. I finally stopped dreaming about missing meetings, phone calls and appointments. The unrushed, slower pace of our new cruising lifestyle provided time for thought and reflection. I learned to sit still and enjoy daydreaming or reading a good book without feeling guilty about wasting time. I allowed my mind to wander.

The lesson prompted one of the first shifts in my perspective of life--a flicker of recognition that, in times of quiet thoughtfulness, I was more open to receive creative ideas, inspiration and higher levels of awareness. Some people call it meditation; others call it prayer or Zen. I believe it was the beginning of my journey to rediscover my soul, my spirit and to find an inner power of healing when I needed it most.

Chapter 3
Canada To The Chesapeake Bay

August 1996

A bright, red school bus-turned-diner served fish and chips by the boardwalk in the town of Killarney on the Canadian shore of Lake Huron. Behind the diner a fishing boat tied up to the pier. Still dressed in their yellow, suspendered foul-weather pants, the fishermen unload tubs of fish from their boats and carried them in the back door of the bus. No question that the fish served there was fresh! Ken and I tied *Iniki* up along the boardwalk and joined the line in front of the diner's "Order Here" window. It felt good to be off the boat and stretch our legs so, after our tasty lunch, we wandered around town.

On Channel Street I read a hand made sign staked in the front yard of a neatly kept house: "Vegetables From Garden For Sale". *Mmmmm....I'd love some nice home grown vegetables.* A scrawled note taped to the front door read: "I'm out back in the garden". We circled around the house past some gorgeous flower beds to find the vegetable garden. An old man appeared from of the shed.

"Hi!" I greeted

"Hey!" was his reply.

"Are you the person selling vegetables?" I inquired.

"Yup, what little that's left. I've got some lettuce, some small beets and an odd onion."

That phrase, "an odd onion", made me smile. Something about the man reminded me of my Grandpa DeYoung, who was also a great gardener when he was alive. I looked around and noticed there was not a weed in sight. I commented on his beautiful flowers but the old man, Alvin was his name, was not very talkative and he seemed to move in slow motion. Pleasant memories of my grandfather came to me in a rush as I watched Alvin's familiar mannerisms.

Ken kept asking Alvin questions as he snipped lettuce, basil, and parsley, and pulled an odd onion for us. I mentioned that we lived on a sailboat and were just passing through. Alvin paused, and then offered, "There's a man in town

20

who sailed from here all the way to Sweden and back. The boat is down in the harbor."

We paid Alvin for his vegetables. He asked me if I would like some flowers. He cut a bouquet of white mini-mums for me and said they would last for a week or more--a small gift from dear, old Alvin. It made my day.

Sailing east out of Killarney we entered Georgian Bay. We thought it would be fun to explore the narrow canoe paths that meander through the Thirty Thousand Islands area along the coast. The draft on *Iniki* was only 4.5 feet allowing us to get through the shallow sections along that wild and scenic route. Twisting around rocks and islands, the winding channel required some very careful maneuvering. We passed by Fox Island, went around Vixen Island and through Hangdog Passage. I loved the Disneyland-like ride but it was a bit of a nightmare for Captain Ken at the helm. He juggled flip charts, reading glasses, sunglasses and binoculars to follow the numbered markers. To miss a marker, or pass on the wrong side of one, could have put *Iniki* on the rocks. I kept a vigilant watch on the bow to help steer us through the obstacle course.

A couple days later we found ourselves in a popular cottage area. I took the helm while Ken went below. I guess my attention drifted, distracted by a soaring, bald eagle or something. Somehow, I got us into a shallow rocky area with no markers in sight. *Oops!* Ken was a little upset with me. Looking for a way out without running aground we saw a tall, lean woman with long, blond hair standing on a boulder, hands on hips, watching the crazy sailboat that wasn't where it was supposed to be. She was completely naked. Ken verified that fact with the binoculars. Apparently, he needed a second and third look just to be sure. Then, alas, she dove into the water and disappeared like a mirage. We found our way safely back to the marked channel. Ken decided he wasn't that mad about the detour after all.

August 16, 1996

We stopped for fuel in San Souci only to discover that their pump wasn't working. We kept our fingers crossed hoping we would reach South Bay Cove Marina in Honey Harbor without running out of diesel. We coasted into the fuel dock on little more than fumes. The handsome, young dockhand grabbed our lines and greeted us, "I almost forgot what a sailboat looked like." I looked around and saw only big powerboats on the docks. "But don't worry! You are welcome here. We always like to have a couple sailboats in the marina to take the lightning strikes!" he quipped, passing the fuel hose over the lifelines to Ken.

We met Barry, the marina owner, that afternoon. He generously handed us the keys to his suburban to do errands in town. He also shared some good information about where to go to prepare *Iniki* for the Trent-Severn Waterway. The mast would have to come down and a cradle built to hold it securely on deck in order to pass through the locks and bridges along the waterway.

August 20, 1996

We entered the Trent-Severn, known locally as the "Scratch and Dent". The waterway, connecting Georgian Bay to Lake Ontario, is 240 miles of canals, rivers and lakes. There are 60 bridges and 45 locks of all shapes and sizes, from small gates opened by hand to railway lifts that went up and over highways! The highest was a hydraulic lift that raised us sixty-five feet. We motored through the picturesque Kawartha Lakes region and continued on into rolling green farm country. The air was filled with that unmistakable aroma of livestock. Around the next bend several healthy looking Holsteins were at the water's edge, necks stretched out for a drink from the river.

A few marinas were available along the way but usually we simply tied up at a lock for the night. The lockmasters rarely bothered to collect a fee from us. Often it was just a short walk to find a little town that seemed lost in time, as if the residents, who loyally remained, hoped for a return to the former days of prosperity when the lumber mills flourished along the rivers.

Trent-Seven Waterway, Canada

Trent-Seven Waterway, Canada

Big Chute Railway Lock

September 7, 1996

Gray clouds and drizzling rain persisted all day. We approached lock #39, the first in a series of three manually operated locks. Each lock raised us a mere 14 feet and they were about ½ mile apart. Not many boats were on the move that dreary Saturday so Brian, a second-generation lock operator, had time to chat with us. He asked if we would deliver some tomatoes, onions and cucumbers to Max, the operator of lock #37 since we were headed that direction. Max needed the fresh vegetables for a batch of chili he was making.

"No problem!" I said. Brian handed us some extra cucumbers and nice, fat tomatoes to keep for ourselves. Max was happy to get the veggies to complete his chili and insisted on giving us a jar of his homemade salsa. What a deal!

September 14, 1996

Hints of yellow and red in the trees foretold the change of seasons to come. The apple trees along the riverbanks were loaded with ripe, red fruit. I love autumn but that was a reminder to keep moving south toward warmer latitudes.

We endured several days of rain by the time we reached the double locks at Healey Falls. The lockmasters there informed us that lock #16 and #17 were closed. The water level was near flood stage because of all the recent rain (part of the far reaching weather effect of Hurricane Fran out in the Atlantic). Consequently, the locks closed and the dam was opened to run off the excess water, which resulted in a very swift and treacherous river.

"It could be up to ten days before we get the OK to open again." the bearded man in brown uniform told us with regret. *Great! Only 36 miles from the open water of Lake Ontario and we're trapped.* We soon discovered that we were stuck in the middle of nowhere. There wasn't a thing we could do about it so we got out the fishing poles and fished. The nearest town was twelve miles away. Dave and Rick, the lockmeisters, as Ken called them, were nice enough to offer to pick up eggs, milk or whatever we needed on their way in to work. When I baked bread, I made an extra loaf for our gate-keepers. One morning Dave even brought us some pickerel and ground moose meat from his freezer at home.

"Moose meat?" I questioned skeptically. My face must have revealed my apprehension because he quickly assured me it was better than beef and very lean. I cooked it in some chili and it was quite good.

Our "stuck" sailboat became sort of a novelty to the folks in the area. People would stop by daily to see if we were still there. One thoughtful, elderly couple seemed to be worried about us and drove me to town one day to get groceries. Another day, after returning from a walk, we found a bag in our cockpit. It contained two newspapers and a Cruising World Magazine with a note: "Thought you might need some reading material. If there is anything else I can do for you, just call." *What a friendly place to be held hostage!*

September 22, 1996

On our eighth day at Healey Falls Dave came over to our boat. "We got the green light to open the locks tomorrow," he reported. "If you get an early start you might make it all the way through to lock #1 in one day."

I took pictures to remember our entrapment and asked the guys to sign my travel journal. I kept a separate book with photos of people we met along our way.

Rick wrote:

> "Ken & Jane, you both have been great folks to
> have captured for a week. No whining, bitching,
> etc. Most folks who are delayed for a half an hour
> freak on us. We wish you well!!
> Rick Foster, Lock Operator, Healey Falls, Ontario,
> Canada"

The following morning Dave and Rick both arrived earlier than usual. Rick brought us some more fish and Bush Beef (moose). *Iniki* slowly dropped about 25 feet as the water drained from the lock. The gates opened and Ken exited the lock. I looked up behind us and waved goodbye as Ken gave a farewell blast with the air horn. A response boomed over the loud speaker: "Hey, cut out the racket! Have a safe trip, guys."

We suspected that our new friends called the locks down the line to us get through as quickly as possible because the last crew actually waited for us about fifteen minutes after normal closing time. We finally made it to the Bay of Quinte on Lake Ontario! We anchored for the night and prepared to cross the lake to New York State.

September 24, 1996

Our first attempt to cross Lake Ontario from Trenton on the Canadian side to New York State was aborted when the waves proved to be larger than reported. The jostling action was too hard on the creaking wood cradle that held the mast of our sailboat horizontally over the deck. With every creak and moan from the wood I feared the mast would crash down on our heads or slide into the water. That was silly, of course, since it was lashed down but I worried about it nonetheless.

We altered course and anchored in a small bay off Main Duck Island. The next morning we set out again under sunny skies. The light wind and minimal seas provided a much smoother ride back into U.S. waters. We arrived in Oswego, New York by 5:30PM.

The Oswego River carried us to the Erie Canal and more locks and bridges. The days began to get chilly and we were now in the company of many other boats also heading south. The Mohawk River joined the Erie Canal System for several miles. My mind conjured up images of fur traders and native Indian tribes of a bygone era as we traveled down the same river plied by those early Americans. The river flowed past crumbling ruins of old canal locks, ancient overgrown cemeteries, rocky cliffs, hillside farm pastures, and small towns decorated in fall foliage. In five days we reached the last lock in Troy, New York. We'd been through 75 locks altogether and were relieved to be done with them. It was an exciting prospect to get the mast back in place so we could be a sailboat again.

On the crisp, clear morning of October 2, 1996 we stepped the mast at Hop-O-Nose Marina in Catskill Creek, New York. We sailed down the Hudson River by lavish estates set high upon the bluffs along the river, and past West Point Academy. From the Catskills to Poughkeepsie, Tarrytown to The Big Apple, the open spaces filled in and vanished, as we got closer to New York City.

Staying at the obscure live-aboard marina at the 79th Street Yacht Basin for a bargain $10.00 per night, we found ourselves in a great location on the Upper West Side of Manhattan. There was a wonderful bagel shop in the neighborhood where I stopped daily and had fun strolling through Zabar's, a famous giant gourmet store full of international culinary delights.

October 8, 1996

For a few days Ken watched the threatening path of tropical storm, Josephine in the Atlantic Ocean. The storm gained strength as it moved in a northerly direction up the Eastern seaboard. Gale force winds howled through

New York City with heavy rain. We saw big ships head up the Hudson River seeking protection and cringed at the sight of capsized pleasure boats getting swept downstream.

The night was long and uncomfortable. I was nauseous from the rolling motion but *Iniki* weathered it just fine, thanks to the gargantuan fender loaned to us by the dock master who referred to the storm as a baby nor'easter. *Baby?* The storm delay gave us a chance to see a Broadway show and visit with friends in the city that we hadn't seen in years. When the weather settled we got our boat ready for our very first ocean passage.

Sailing past the twin towers New York City

October 11, 1996

Leaving New York City through the New York Harbor was both thrilling and stressful. It was thrilling to sail our own boat past the profusion of steel and concrete; the Empire State Building, the World Trade Center and Ellis Island. The ultimate was sailing by the Statue of Liberty! I imagined all the millions of immigrants who laid eyes on that symbol of freedom when they arrived, full of hope, to begin a new life. I was overcome with a sense of patriotism that left a lump in my throat.

Just then the Circle Line Ferry raced past us. Its wake rocked *Iniki* and jolted my attention back to the whirlwind of activity all around us. Freighters, tankers, barges, military ships and cruise ships moved up and down the main channel through the harbor. Twenty others were anchored. Tour helicopters buzzed around and commercial airline jumbo jets circled in a landing pattern for JFK Airport. Red and green buoys seemed to be everywhere marking secondary channels that branched off in various directions. Commercial fishing trawlers and about a hundred small fishing boats added to the chaos--just your average day in New York City. I was a nervous wreck. Ken loved it.

We followed the Ambrose Channel past Sandy Hook and *Iniki* lunged ahead into the Atlantic Ocean. The plan was to stop in Atlantic City. However, once we covered a few miles Ken listened to the weather forecast and did some revised time, speed and distance calculations. "Jane, conditions are good and we're moving along fine. I think we should keep on going all night. We can be in Cape May, New Jersey by morning."

As the sun went down we toasted our first day in the Atlantic with a glass of wine. "Cheers! Here's to another milestone in our adventure!" Ken said, excitedly.

The two of us felt exhilarated. *We are sailing in the ocean. We're really doing this!*

After a quick supper I bundled up against the cold night air and donned my safety harness to take the first night watch. We reefed the main sail before Ken went below to get some rest. We arrived at Cape May, New Jersey at dawn as planned. Dozens of fishing boats headed out to sea as we entered the inlet. It felt like we were driving the wrong way on a one-way street. Anchored in the harbor, we grabbed a few hours of sleep, and then went ashore to sample the seafood at The Lobster House on the waterfront.

Lobster traps were stacked high outside the restaurant. Inside the walls, ceilings and corners were filled with all things nautical--fishing nets, buoys, mounted fish, oars, lanterns, and wooden ship parts. It was a very "salty" atmosphere. We ate peel-n-eat shrimp, steamed clams, mussels, and crab soup all washed down with ice-cold beer. At the restaurant's carry out market we picked up some fresh dolphin fillets and a bag of small lobster tails to take back to the boat.

We needed to leave before sun up the next morning, at low tide, in order to take advantage of the extra 2 knot current up the Delaware Bay. The bay can be quite nasty if you don't coordinate your trip with the tides. Ken did his homework and we had a fast sail with the winds and currents in our favor. Once through the C&D Canal (no locks!) we immediately discovered the lure and appeal of the Chesapeake Bay.

The fall colors were brilliant along the Sassafrass and Chester Rivers. It was my first visit to that area and I would have loved to linger a while. I wanted to explore every river and creek eating my fill of the fresh seafood that was available everywhere--crab cakes, crab chowder, steamed crab, clams, shrimp and lobster. I was in heaven!

October 15, 1996

When we arrived in Baltimore thirty old wooden schooners gathered for The Great Chesapeake Bay Schooner Race from Baltimore to Norfolk. Several of them were still working oyster boats. Under sail they were a grand sight to see. We had a few repairs to attend to on *Iniki* and Annapolis was the logical place to do that. Once the depth gauge and autopilot were fixed we left to eagerly explore some more gunk holes. We gradually moved south and discovered some lovely secluded coves to spend our nights. One such hide-away was up the Wye River. Huge flocks of swans gathered along the banks. We turned into Lloyd's Creek, a branch off the river, and anchored.

Pretty and secluded? Yes. Peaceful? No! The farm fields on both sides of the creek were filled with Canada geese. One moment they foraged on the ground. Then, for no apparent reason, they took to flight and blackened the sky as they circled and landed again. They never settled down. Their boisterous honking was non-stop the remainder of the afternoon and continued into the evening.

After dinner that night Ken challenged me to a game of backgammon. I was down two games when I noticed that the table wasn't level.

"Ken, why are we leaning to port?" I asked.

"You live on a boat, woman! What do you expect?" he quickly replied as he rolled doubles again. *Hmmmmm. This isn't right. Why isn't he listening to me?*

Within 15 to 20 minutes the dice slid right off the table. We were practically on our backs as we sat on the settee and laughed. "I *told* you!"

The tide went out and left us on the muddy bottom in only 3 feet of water. Obviously, we were not accustomed to dealing with tides. According to the tide tables the next high tide was a 5am but we woke up at 7am-- too late! We remained hard aground until late afternoon. The severe angle of *Iniki* lying on her side sure made it difficult to move about the boat. Eventually, we floated off with no damage and with just enough time to find deeper water to re-anchor before it got dark again.

The guide book said, "You are not adventurous enough in your exploring if you don't go aground a few times every year." (Oh, yea, that's it! We meant to do that!)

Along the Choptank River we saw local watermen tonging for clams or oysters. We listened to them talking to each other over the VHF radio. I know they were speaking English but I could not understand a word they said.

Tangier Island, Chesapeake Bay

Chapter 4
The Dismal Swamp to the Florida Keys

November 5, 1996

An impressive display of gray Navy battleships, aircraft carriers and submarines lay in port as we sailed through Norfolk, Virginia. My husband was ecstatic to learn that a brand new destroyer, the S.S. Cole, was open to the public that week so we paused long enough to take the tour. Thoroughly impressed with the high-tech weaponry and service men and women aboard, I was glad they were all on our side.

South of Norfolk Ken and I steered *Iniki* off the main Intracoastal Waterway to venture down the Dismal Swamp route to Elizabeth City, North Carolina. Elizabeth City became well known among boaters because of the "Rose Buddies", gray haired gentlemen who drive their golf carts down to the city dock each day to greet the boaters who stop for the night. As the self-elected welcoming committee for the town, the Rose Buddies arrive about 4:30 in the afternoon to charm the women with red rose buds and serve cheese, crackers, wine and beer while they chat with visitors passing through.

We were five months into our voyage by the time we traveled through North Carolina. Unblemished by mishaps, *Iniki* still looked brand new. But a late afternoon storm caught us in the Pungo River right before we reached River Forest Marina in Bellhaven, NC. The teak suffered a gouge and the bow light was bent as we struggled to dock *Iniki* in fifty-knot winds and driving rain. The boat bucked and rolled in the churning water and caught the anchor under the T-dock. I stood helpless on the bow in my foul weather gear and life jacket. With Ken at the helm I felt responsible, somehow, to protect the rest of the boat from damage. *What am I supposed to do to help? Fend off the pier?* I quickly realized that it was foolish to risk a crushed arm, or worse. The anchor pounded against the underside of the pier and popped up two wood planks. *How can I safely push the pulpit out from under the dock?* The wind howled. Ken had the boat in reverse but the dinghy was caught between the stern and a piling acting like a fender and prevented any backward movement. *I need to get off the boat to tie the lines.* I looked at the height of the pier and the wild motion of the boat. *No way!* As the thought went through my mind the dockhand arrived to help us. *Oh, thank you!*

The rain pelted us with a force that almost hurt. I tossed my new best friend a mid-ship spring line followed by bow and stern lines.

"You're safe. I gottcha now." The local man hollered over the wind as he caught and secured our lines. "Don't worry about the dock. That ain't nothin' to fix."

Once we finally got off the boat onto the pier I wanted to hug that man. Ken showed his appreciation with a hearty handshake and a generous tip. The nasty squall passed and Ken and I warmed up next to the fire in the marina restaurant where I calmed my rattled nerves with a double gin & tonic. Ken reassured me that the rub rail on the boat was easy to repair.

"Jane, you did a great job with the lines. I'm proud of you. Don't even think about getting yourself between the boat and the dock in those conditions. Your safety is more important than a piece of wood."

I was certainly glad we saw eye to eye on the safety issue. After I had time to think about it, I was impressed with my husband's boat handling skills in those adverse conditions. It's one thing to talk about what to do in a storm. It's quite another to actually get through it. Hopefully there won't be a next time, but if there is, I will be a little less scared knowing Ken's ability to handle the situation.

The Intracoastal Waterway passed through the war training zone of Lejeune Marine Base in North Carolina. There are signal signs posted at the perimeter to indicate whether or not it is safe to proceed. Red lights mean the area is closed due to explosions or other live ammunitions used in training missions. When we approached we saw no danger warnings so we continued down the river with caution. Two camouflaged amphibian tanks appeared out of the woods and crossed the river right behind us. A helicopter circled very close to our boat. Ken gave a friendly wave but the soldiers were all business.

Iniki ran the gauntlet unharmed and stopped for the night in a lagoon around the next bend in the river. In the morning we woke up to find the beach lined with tanks from one end to the other. Their turret guns looked like they were aimed directly at us. *Yikes!* I passed the binoculars to Ken and urged, "Let's get out of here before we become the target and imaginary enemy in their Marine games!"

Exiting the "war zone" we happily found ourselves back in the remote, coastal, low country where marsh grass the color of cinnamon and ochre spread as far as I could see. Tall prehistoric looking wood storks stood on the riverbanks poking their long bills into the muck. Mallard ducks tipped upside down and waved their feet in the air while they ate off the bottom. Colorful wood ducks, mergansers and cute, little buffle heads swam and splashed in and out of the reeds. When we began to see pelicans and dolphins daily I knew we were making progress in our passage south.

December 11, 1996

On Dataw Island in South Carolina the marina manager lent us his old Cadillac to go to town for a few supplies. The car was falling apart and the headlights didn't work so I kept my fingers crossed that the dilapidated Caddy would make it back to the marina before dark.

In town at the 24-Hour Plaza Ken pointed out a big, three-gallon jar of pickled pigs feet on the deli counter. They looked like some ghastly biology lab specimen. The man behind the counter told Ken it was a fresh jar (as if that was the clincher to entice us to purchase a few).

Ken inquired, "Do *you* eat them?"

The reply, "Yea, I've ate a foot", came in a barely understandable, raspy southern drawl that sent Ken into fit of laughter.

"Well, how do they taste?" Ken asked.

"Knuckley!" croaked the clerk, "but they make good emergency provisions because they don't never go bad." We declined the offer to taste them for ourselves and bought a bag of potato chips instead. The burly, red headed fellow followed us out the front door of the store. He hitched up his pants and offered, "If y'all get your courage up, come on back. We're open 24 hours."

"We'll keep that in mind." Ken chuckled with a wave of his hand.

"I know we're still in the United States," I mentioned to Ken as we arrived safely back at the marina, "but it sure seems like a foreign country to me."

When there was no educational interaction with the local population, our days blurred together. Pushing hard to cover as many miles as possible each day, we got under way in morning before daylight and anchored just before sundown. We ate, slept, woke up and did it all over again.

Wood stork - South Carolina lo.

December 16, 1996

Finally, *Iniki* crossed the Florida State line—cause for celebration! Ken went below to whip up some Pina Coladas in the blender. *So where is the warm, sunny Florida weather the tourist board brags about?* I still wore gloves because it was freezing cold. We had two daughters arriving for a holiday visit aboard our sailboat and I wished for hot weather for them.

Our daughter, Kassie was flying in from Chicago after her first semester of college. Tina, who was two years older, would fly in from California where she lived. Two extra bodies and two extra duffle bags make a huge difference on a narrow 34-foot sailboat but both girls adapted well to the cramped quarters with minimal complaints. Both of them had been on chartered sailing vacations with us in the Virgin Islands, and both had boating experience from summer camp and Outward Bound. Their main concern, as I knew it would be, was acquiring an awesome tan before returning home.

After rush, rush, rushing down the east coast, Ken and I looked forward to their visit and were ready for fun. We slowed the pace down and enjoyed a week-long cruise through the Florida Keys. It was easy to slide into that laid back "island feeling". The group swam, fished, explored and ate lobster. Bob Marley music played non-stop on the stereo to keep things "irie". By the time we left the remote, uninhabited islands in the Middle Keys, Tina and Kassie were ready for the party atmosphere of Key West. The performing artists on Mallory Square at sunset and a cheeseburger in paradise at Jimmy Buffet's Margaritaville restaurant on Duvall Street provided the perfect finale to their vacation.

January 10, 1997

The weather deteriorated the day after the girls left and subjected us to eight chilly, rainy days. That was OK. It was nice to stay in one spot for the week. We had no TV or VCR on board so we read tons of books. Most marinas have a "Take One-Leave One" bookshelf that we frequently perused. We also traded books with other boaters. The further down island we went in the Caribbean, the more important the books became. Sometimes the choices were dog-eared and required bug spray before we brought them aboard our boat. But we gladly went to the trouble just to insure sufficient reading material was available at anchor. Many books had the names of other cruisers written inside the cover and it was fun to see how far the books had traveled.

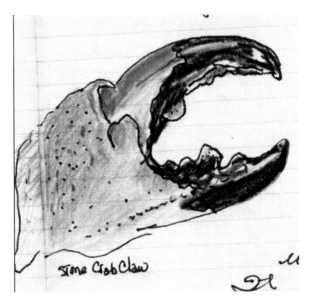

Stone Crab Claw

During our stay in Key West we were anchored in Flamingo Bay. A few crab pots were scattered through the area. There was one crab pot close to our boat, at times, depending on the way we swung around the anchor with the tides. No one ever checked it the entire time we were there. The morning we prepared to leave, Ken talked about how we would get the two anchors up since the lines were all twisted. It was going to take some extra time and maneuvering to get them back in the boat. I listened to the plan and then asked, "Now what about that crab pot that's next to the boat?"

"Don't worry about it", Ken said, dismissing my concern. "Just follow my simple instructions".

He didn't even bother to look to see how close the pot was. Fuming behind the wheel I followed his hand signals and changed gears: forward-neutral-forward to port....CLUNK-CLUNK! In less than thirty seconds the crab pot line was fouled in our prop!

I barely repressed the urge to scream out, *I told you so! Why didn't you listen to me, you big jerk!* But I bit my tongue and sat smugly silent. I know timing is everything. I'll get my licks in later.

Ken covered his embarrassment with anger that festered as he cut, untangled and hauled up the slimy line and heavy crab trap. A jumble of stone crabs climbed all over each other inside the smelly wooden trap.

"For all that trouble we're having crab for lunch!" Ken snarled as he dumped the crabs into a bucket.

Feeling slightly guilty about trap robbing I glanced around for witnesses before I broke off only one claw from each crab. I tossed the feisty crabs overboard knowing they could survive while the second claw grew back. Captain Ken, still quite crabby, grumbled something about me being a do-gooder. *Well I'd rather be a do-gooder than a pompous know-it-all who can't admit he should have listened to his wife.*

In the future I found numerous occasions to sling that line, 'Just follow my simple instructions', back at my husband to elicit the humbling effect intended. I milked it for all it was worth.

January 24, 1997

On our sail back to Miami from Key West we stopped for the night in an area marked on the chart as "Cow Pen Anchorage" near Islamorada in the Middle Keys. We had an excellent sail and were settled in our cockpit gazing at a Monet sunset against a dappled sky. I let out a sigh of appreciation, "This is what it's all about!"

My soul mate agreed. "And it's only the beginning. We aren't even to the good part yet." Ken joked.

I chuckled and remembered last summer in Canada... I commented on the beautiful scenery to another boater who told me, "This isn't even the good part. Wait 'til you get to...". I wondered if that person ever enjoyed where he *was* or if he was always chasing after someplace better. I was learning to live in the moment.

Soon the sun disappeared behind the mangroves leaving streaks of pink and purple. A bright, full moon rose in the east over the still water. A line of white ibis flew overhead returning to roost. There was beauty in every direction. Another contented sigh. For me, that closeness to Nature was one of the best things about the whole voyage. I wanted to remember that sight forever and be able to recall the feeling of peace and tranquility. Little did I know how important that mental image would be to me two years later, when my body would be poked and prodded by doctors and technicians in cold sterile offices in Chicago. In order to stay calm and relaxed through those medical treatments, I would close my eyes and mentally transport myself back to the serenity of the islands.

February 1, 1997

After much research Ken ordered a wind generator and watermaker that we had installed in Miami. We provisioned for six months—stocking up on items that were hard to find or very expensive in the islands, like zip lock bags, pop, beer, film, paper towels, etc. We were ready for the Bahamas! Ken listened to the weather three times a day. He had sailed across the Gulf Stream before and knew it could be awful if the wind and sea conditions were ignored. I was anxious to leave but I wanted a nice smooth ride. Ken, aware that I was still a novice at ocean passages, did not want to scare me or turn me off to sailing altogether with a terrible trip. So, we waited for the right weather forecast. Moving across the bay we staged ourselves in No Name Harbor at the south end of Key Biscayne and waited a few more days before our break came.

February 22, 1997

We left No Name Harbor shortly before midnight. I heard so many horror stories from other cruisers about bad Gulf Stream crossings, that I was a quite apprehensive as we headed out to sea that night, even though I didn't admit it. But there was no need to worry. It was a beautiful clear night with a full moon, a light breeze and small swells. On my watch at 3:00am I was startled out of my wandering thoughts by an unmistakable, loud blow of air. I looked to port in time to see a tall black fin slowly sink below the surface not more than 100 feet away. I gasped and strained to see through the darkness.

"Whale!" I cried out excitedly and woke Ken. He banged his head on the dodger when he hurried up on deck, cursing as he looked around. Sadly, we never saw it surface again. I flipped through my identification book and recognized the dorsal fin of an Orca or Killer Whale. Seeing a whale, or at least part of one, was absolutely thrilling but also a wee bit spooky.

"I wish you could have seen it, Ken. It was *so* close. I wonder how many huge things are swimming under us at this very moment. Wouldn't you love to have a peek under the surface and be able to see for miles at a time?" I chattered on in my excitement. Ken rubbed his throbbing head and just wanted to go back to sleep. Images of whales and other monsters of the deep fueled my imagination for the remainder of my watch.

At dawn the rising sun backlit the islands as we approached creating unique silhouettes on the horizon. "Welcome to the Bahamas!" Ken said with his best Bahamian accent as he gave me a "high five".

"We did it!" I replied. "You picked a perfect window to cross the Gulf Stream and your crew loves you for it."

It took us 8.5 hours to sail to Cat Cay where we checked in with Customs and Immigration at the marina. A man in a crisp white uniform helped us with our lines. He laughed when Ken greeted him, "You're my first Bahamian!" After clearing in we sailed across the Grand Bahama Bank and "The Tongue of the Ocean". This was *big* fish territory so naturally we had a fishing line out. We got a huge strike that nearly ran out all the line on our heavy-duty reel. The sailboat rolled in the chop and I struggled to keep my balance and the rod tip up. Ken gripped the wheel with one hand and hung on to me with the other to keep me onboard. My arm muscles shook with exhaustion. I longed to catch a glimpse of what felt like a trophy fish. But *Iniki* wasn't designed for championship deep-sea fishing. We really didn't want to catch a 1000-pound Marlin anyway. All we wanted was enough fish for dinner. Suddenly, the line went slack and I knew I lost it.

February 25, 1997

Thirty-six miles west of Nassau, at the south end of the Berry Islands is a place called Chubb Cay. In Chubb Cay we gained some valuable local knowledge from an expert conch fisherman—how to clean and prepare conch. The skinny conch man showed Ken how to get the reluctant critter out of its beautiful shell and I learned how to prepare it. The key to tender conch is to sufficiently "bruise it"—the local lingo for pounding the heck out of it before it is cooked.

Since we completed "Conch-101" we could confidently explore the remote Out Islands of the Bahamas without fear of starvation. Equipped with our new knowledge, we could always rustle up some conch if we failed to catch fish. It was easy and we didn't even have to sneak up on them. The animals certainly weren't going to bolt and run away. Now *that* was peace of mind!

Ken Conquers Conch

The Conchman in Chubb Cay

Chapter 5
The Bahamas to Puerto Rico

March 12, 1997

"Blue blue-sail on through
Green green-nice and clean
Brown brown-run aground!"

This helpful ditty from the guidebook was my mantra to avoid coral heads throughout the Bahamas. On all our passages, as we hopped down the Exuma chain, I positioned myself on the bow to help read the shallow water in our path. Then, when it was time to anchor, Ken and I switched places. I took over the helm while Ken handled the anchor and chain.

During the months of March and April long-tailed, white Tropic Birds return from the Sargasso Sea to nest in the Exuma Islands. When we approached Shroud Cay the graceful birds were chirping and swooping through the air as they performed their mating rituals. I loved watching their synchronized acrobatics high above us.

"Jane, watch *me* not the birds!" my annoyed partner reminded me when I missed his hand signals during our anchoring process. Hand signals eliminate any need to shout, whether it is to be heard over the wind or due to an angry tirade which the rest of the anchorage would rather not hear.

"Oh, sorry," I said and momentarily refocused my attention on Ken, although I was defiantly thinking, *I can do the anchoring drill and watch the birds at the same time.* I indulged his discourse on the importance of communication and teamwork on a boat. *Oh, for Pete's sake! At the moment there's no emergency but there IS a unique opportunity to view a rare display of nature.* "OK. Yes, you're right," I sighed, knowing he wasn't really mad. He knew I always noticed the birds and wanted to identify them, something I picked up from my mother.

I kept my eyes on the boss. Standing at the bow Ken patted his backside, and then flashed five fingers four times. Translation: reverse throttle at 500, 1000,

1500 then 2000 rpms to back down on the anchor and bury it in the sandy bottom. Ken took a bearing to be certain we weren't dragging.

"We're there, J-bird," he said using his pet name for me. "You can kill the engine."

I coiled the sheets, put on the sail cover and settled down with the binoculars to watch the graceful white birds with the long flowing tails. Ken marked the logbook, poured drinks and joined me in the cockpit for happy hour's airborne entertainment.

March 20, 1997

The south anchorage of Wardrick Wells is part of the Bahamas Land and Sea Park, which means that spear fishing is prohibited. Mooring cans are provided in order to protect the turtle grass from anchor damage. After we picked up an available mooring I hailed the park ranger on the VHF radio to inquire about the fee.

"Wardrick Wells Ranger Station, Wardrick Wells Ranger Station. This is sailing vessel, *Iniki.*"

"*Iniki,* Ranger Station. Go ahead." came the response.

"Good morning. We just arrived and picked up a mooring in the south anchorage. Can you tell me what the fee is and how we pay it?"

"Roger, Captain. It's $15.00 for two nights. Just leave it in the mailbox on the beach."

"Roger. We will leave it in the mailbox. Thank you. *Iniki* is clear, standing by Channel 16." Hanging up the mike I turned to Ken and said, "That's a mellow island attitude for you. I love it!"

We had a perfect white sand beach all to ourselves in that peaceful spot. Exploring a bit, we discovered a little trail through the palm trees and scrub brush lined with old conch shells. Brown lizards with curled up tails darted about on the ground. Overhead, mockingbirds sang their hearts out. The path led to a fresh water well at the center of the island. Someone painted the word, "Laundromat", on one of the rocks at the edge of the well.

Our private beach resembled the tropical paradise of my dreams and we enjoyed a luxuriously lazy afternoon. The warm sun, the sound of the surf crashing in the distance and the gentle lapping of the water on the sand nearly lulled me to sleep. A spotted eagle ray suddenly leaped out of the water and landed with a loud smack. Just above the waterline a conch inched ever so slowly along the sand. *Where are you heading?* I wondered, amused by the sight. *Don't you know you are supposed to be IN the water not out roaming the beach?*

Later that evening, after dinner on the boat, I threw some food scraps overboard. Instantly, a mouth full of teeth erupted from the water and gulped the scraps with lightning speed. I heard myself scream and Ken hurried up from below. I threw another tidbit overboard so Ken could also meet the "jaws". The ten-year-old boy inside my middle-aged husband tied a rope around a cleaned off T-bone, and then dangled it in the water. "Let's see if he goes after this," he said with a mischievous spark in his eye. Nothing happened. I laughed, secretly pleased. They don't get that big by being stupid, as the saying goes. Ken threw another unattached bone and got an instant reaction...strike-splash-gone! That wise old 'cuda hovered in the shade under our boat for two days.

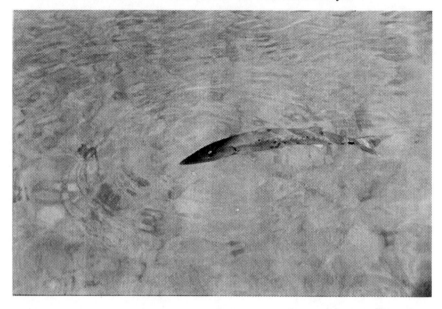

Barracuda

For cruisers, the VHF and/or Single Side Band Radio on their vessel serves as the main line of communication with other boaters and marine related businesses on land. Wherever there are large clusters of cruisers there will be a "Net" on the radio in the morning. There are wide range nets on the SSB radio. For example, on the NW Caribbean Net, cruisers check in from Jamaica, Cuba, Cayman Islands, Mexico, Belize, Guatemala, Honduras and Florida. On the Panama Net, boats hail from Cartegena, Colombia to the Galapagos Islands in the Pacific. It's an excellent way to get actual, real-time wind and wave conditions to supplement the NOAA weather faxes. There are also local nets for particular harbors. Local VHF nets might sound something like this:

> **Net Control (NC)**: "Good Morning. Today is Tuesday, March 20, 1997. My name is Joe aboard *Wind Song* and I'll be your net controller for today. The purpose of this net is to provide information and assistance to cruisers. This is a controlled net so please wait to be recognized. Now let's all listen carefully for any medical, emergency or priority traffic. That traffic and that traffic only, come now. (Pause) Nothing heard, that's always good. New arrivals--are there any new arrivals who would like to say hello? Come now."

Boater: Ken keys the mike and checks in. *"Iniki"*

NC: *"Iniki*! Go ahead."

Boater: "This is the sailing vessel, *Iniki.* My name is Ken and my wife is Jane. We sailed from Chicago and are bound for Venezuela."

NC: "Welcome! Any other new arrivals? Departures? Is anyone leaving who wants to say goodbye? Let's move on to general check in, one at a time, please."

(At this time all boaters who care to, check in and are acknowledged by the control.) This is more important than merely being a way to meet people. It serves as a location trail. Should a boat be reported missing, rescue attempts can track the last known location through the net's records.

NC: "Weather. *Wind Dancer,* are you ready with the weather?"

Boater: "This is Tom, on *Wind Dancer.* The weather fax didn't come in very clear this morning, but I'll do my best to read it. At 0600, North of 20 degrees North and West of 70 degrees West, winds 10-15 knots, seas 5 feet or less. Tonight, winds East-Southeast 10-15 knots, seas 5 feet or less. Synopsis--no significant features. Outlook through the weekend, little change. (The report would continue in more detail) Any questions?"

NC: "Thanks, Tom. Services wanted or needed, come now."

Boater: *"Island Time"*

Boater: *"Orion".*

NC: "Go ahead, *Island Time"*

Boater: "This is *Island Time.* I have a 15- foot whisker pole for sale. I'll be standing by on channel 68 after the net."

NC: "OK, Anyone needs a whisker pole; contact Island Time on Channel 68. *Orion*, go ahead with your services wanted or needed."

Boater: "This is Jack on *Orion*. Does anyone know where I can find a fuel filter for a 3Jh2E Yanmar diesel engine?"

Boater: "*Crystal*"

NC: "*Crystal*, go"

Boater: "If you walk down the main road from the dinghy dock and turn left past Two Turtles Inn, you will see a little general store. Ask at the counter in the back. If they don't have one, give me a shout. I may have one on board somewhere."

(The net would continue with social announcements, if any)

NC: "Is there anything else for the net, this morning? If not, this net is over and the channel is open for traffic. Have a good day."

Georgetown on Great Exuma Island is one of those popular gathering places for cruisers. It is also known as "Chicken Harbor" because so many boaters heading to the Caribbean get as far as Georgetown, then chicken out and go no further. From Great Exuma the Out Islands of the Bahamas get farther apart and the passages get significantly more challenging. At peak times of the year there can be up to five hundred boats anchored in the spacious harbor at Georgetown. The local community is very gracious and many helpful services are available to the boaters. When we arrived on *Iniki*, the Exuma Market offered mail and email service along with special grocery orders. Mom's Bakery sold fresh bread and other baked goodies every morning on the waterfront. A rake & scrape band played on Tuesdays at Eddie's Clearwater, Wednesday was BBQ night at the Two Turtles Inn and the Peace & Plenty Hotel had specials nightly.

The cruiser's net on the VHF radio lasted over 40 minutes with most of the time spent on social events and organized activities. It seemed to me, that the cruisers who came for the winter months went overboard in their attempts to make that quaint local way of life more like the American suburban culture they left behind. Ambitious organizers announced exercise groups, sing-alongs, Bible studies, book exchanges, video exchanges, and organized hikes. Self-appointed monitors felt it was their duty to remind the rest of us about harbor rules and complained about the no-good yahoo who drove his dinghy too fast through the anchorage the night before. It didn't take long before Ken and I felt the urge to gag at all the silliness. Still, I was drawn in like a daily soap opera. I tuned in every morning for a chuckle while I sipped my coffee.

April 8, 1997

For two weeks the winds cranked out of the east at 20 knots. We waited patiently for a southerly wind shift that would allow us to leave Georgetown. Eventually, we got our break and sailed east to the more remote out-islands. On route from Long Island to Rum Cay we hooked a hefty fish that Ken battled for 40 minutes. He hauled up half of a mangled mahi-mahi. A shark bit off the tail end but there was still plenty to fillet for a couple great meals.

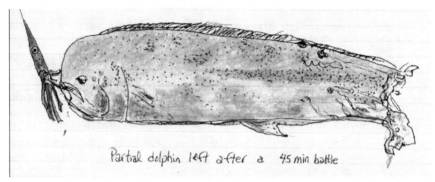

Partial dolphin left after a 45 min battle

Beautiful coral reefs surround Rum Cay. We snorkeled over underwater gardens with massive elk horn coral and purple sea fans waving gracefully in the currents. The winds piped up again so we stayed and enjoyed Rum Cay for a few days. I wanted to call our daughter, Kassie while we were at Rum Cay. A simple telephone call—one of the things I always took for granted in the United States—required extensive effort in the far corners of the Bahamas. First, we had to locate the Batelco Tower. (Clue: look for the highest point on the island) We walked over a mile, climbed to the top of the hill and found only one phone with limited hours of operation. We took our place in the waiting line out in the hot sun. Our turn came thirty minutes later. I gave the phone number to the operator at the switchboard and went into the phone booth. When the phone rang, I picked up the receiver and eagerly anticipated talking to our daughter in college.

"No, Kassie isn't here" her roommate informed me. "Yes, I'll tell her that you called".

It was a long shot to catch Kassie in her dorm room under any circumstances and there was no way she could call us so, whenever possible, we tried to schedule specific times to call. Once we set up a system to send and receive email through our single sideband radio we were able to communicate with everyone regularly. That alleviated my anxiety and guilt about not being accessible to our families.

April 18, 1997

Our passage from Rum Cay to Mayaguana (still part of the Bahamas) was a 28-hour trip. After resting for a day we set sail again for the Turks and Caicos. We had an excellent sail and made great time.

"Why stop?" Ken thought. "We should take advantage of this window."

We sailed on to the Dominican Republic on the island of Hispaniola. Ken and I scheduled regular watches on our overnight passages. One of us was always at the helm. Throughout the day we were flexible, but from sunset to dawn we maintained a three-hour watch. Every five to ten minutes, I did a 360-degree visual sweep of the horizon to watch for ships. We had a metal radar reflector hung below our spreaders so our boat would cause a blip on the radar screens of the ships. I still worried about being run down by the enormous vessels at sea at night.

During the second night of the passage from Mayaguana to the D.R., I was sleeping when the sound of the engine woke me. Worried and not knowing what was happening, I hurried up to the cockpit. At 3:30am Ken spotted a ship on the horizon. He was concerned with the speed at which it approached on a collision course. Ken revved the engine to top speed and turned *Iniki* away from the path of the ship.

It was that high-pitched whine of the engine that scared me out of my berth. I was terrified when I saw how shaken Ken was. He was shining a spot light on our mainsail in an effort to be more visible to the ship, which steamed right past us. It looked gigantic and towered over us.

Rattled, Ken relayed the incident to me, "I'm sure that was a U.S. military ship. It had to be cruising at thirty knots. One minute it was a speck on the horizon and the next it was bearing down on us. Jesus, Mary and Joseph! I thought it was all over!"

The ship appeared and disappeared in less than ten, heart-pounding minutes. I really want to believe our skilled, high-tech Navy saw us on their radar and knew our exact position at all times that night.

April 21, 1997

We approached the northern coast of Hispaniola shortly before dawn. I smelled the island before I could see it. A rich, earthy, damp smell, like a rain forest, overpowered the scent of the sea. As darkness gave way to the new day the mountains of the Dominican Republic materialized out of the haze. I noted the striking difference from the low flat dry islands of the Bahamas. We had only been sailing for two and a half days, hardly a lengthy ocean voyage, yet it was a long sail to me. I imagined that I had the same feelings of excitement and anticipation at the sight of new land, as any explorer before me.

We followed some primitive markers into the snug harbor of Luperon. The bay was completely surrounded by mountains making it a perfect hurricane hole. I was surprised to see about forty sailboats bobbing gently at anchor. Our yellow Q flag (quarantine flag) was raised to announce ourselves as new arrivals to the country and it wasn't long before the local commandant came out to our boat, stamped our papers and collected $20.00 in fees. Then we were free to dinghy to shore to look around.

Harbor in Luperon, Dominican Republic

Baseball game in Luperon

Chickens scurried everywhere in the hot, dusty village. Goats and cows roamed freely. A skinny dog with swollen teats trotted after us, wary of getting too close but ready for any scraps tossed her way. Ken and I walked by a vacant lot where a bunch of boys were playing baseball. We stopped for a minute to watch after we noticed their "sporting equipment". They used a stick for a bat, a piece of cardboard for a mitt and a doll's head was the ball.

"Do you suppose this is how Sammy Sosa's career began?" I marveled.

Unreliable electricity was a normal part of life in Luperon. The villagers didn't have much to call their own but they were always smiling and laughing. Their passion for merengue dancing was evident. Every little town in the Dominican Republic has at least one discotheque. Music played throughout Luperon all day and into the night.

Ken and I wanted to see more of the country. With *Iniki* safely anchored we left the boat for 3 days while a friend kept an eye on her. Accompanied by our good friends Jim and Connie on *Gusteau* who we met in the Bahamas, we took a public bus across the mountainous country to the capital city of Santo Domingo situated on the southern coast. The ticket cost sixty pesos (about $4.00) for the hot, cramped five-hour trip. One young man climbed aboard with a rooster under his arm. Another man got on with a shotgun. The bus driver honked the horn for everything. Beep-beep to another passing bus. Beep-beep to a woman on the side of the road. Beep-beep to pass a car. Beep-beep to friends in town. Beep-beep to a cow in the road--for five hours!

In Santo Domingo we stayed in the quaint Colonial Zone. As we strolled past a cigar making shop across from the main square Ken mentioned the historical significance of the city, in case it escaped the rest of us.

"Do you realize that Christopher Columbus and Sir Francis Drake probably walked along these very cobblestone streets and plazas?"

Ken and I had dinner with our traveling buddies in an unforgettable restaurant across from the oldest cathedral in the western hemisphere. La Briciola Restaurante was set in an open-air courtyard of a 400-year-old building. Bright bougainvilleas and potted palms graced the old stone walls, softly illuminated by hidden spotlights. Overhead, stars twinkled in the clear, night sky. A perfect breeze flickered the candlelight and caressed the edges of our white linen tablecloth. Exceptional food and service matched the magical ambiance. I was in love with the romance of it all. That evening alone was worth the whole bus trip to Santo Domingo.

May 1, 1997

Before we could sail away from Luperon we needed to get diesel fuel. There were no marinas with fuel docks in that primitive area. We made arrangements to have fuel delivered to our boat out in the anchorage. Three guys came out in a small boat carrying three, huge, plastic barrels of diesel. I was grossed out when one of them sucked on the black rubber hose and siphoned the diesel into our jerry cans. Ken then poured the fuel from the jerry cans into our tank through a Baja filter. The primitive process took one full hour to fill our 32-gallon tank and 3 extra jerry cans. You do what you gotta do!

Sailing east along the northern coast of the island of Hispanola during daylight hours is a lesson in futility. Christopher Columbus wrote about the difficulty making headway along that coast in the 1400's and, despite modern technology, the challenges are the same today. Due to a weather phenomenon known as the Katabolic effect, the mountains and capes along the northern coastline of the Dominican Republic produce high winds during the daytime. High winds cause rough seas. It was best to sail at night when the winds, supposedly, subsided and the seas had calmed. So the strategy, suggested in a guidebook written by a man who had sailed the coast many times, was to leave a protected harbor just before sundown to get around the capes and have the anchor down by 11:00am before the winds pipe up once again.

Following the book's advice, we left Luperon at 6:15 am, followed the coastline to Sosua and anchored by 11:30 am. The plan was to leave again at 6 pm after the strong afternoon winds subsided. After a swim and a siesta Ken and I were ready to take off again but we could not get our anchor up. It was stuck, no matter what direction we tugged it. There was about ninety minutes of daylight left. I got out the scuba gear in a hurry and Ken dove down sixty feet to discover the problem. Throughout the entire bay there was only one coral head and we found it! The anchor was buried under it with the rode caught around its edges. While Ken worked underwater, I scurried back and forth on deck between the windlass on the bow and the helm. I had to keep the anchor line loose enough for Ken to untangle it and also keep the boat from drifting back or going to far forward over the line.

With teamwork we managed to free ourselves and departed Sosua as the sun slipped below the horizon. The winds continued to blow 25 knots on the nose all night. So much for *that* theory! On the third day we slogged past the last cape to reach Samana at the eastern end of Hispanola. It had been a tough sail but the lush, undeveloped coastline was a beautiful sight to see. Unfortunately, Samana is notorious for thieves and security problems. The local officials warned us quite matter-of-factly, "Don't leave your outboard motor on your dinghy overnight or it will be gone in the morning." *Why haven't they caught the bandits if it is so obvious? Were the Samana officials in cahoots?*

Ken kept an all night vigil with the deck illuminated and flare guns handy, but no one bothered us. Now we faced another challenge—the infamous Mona Passage.

May 4, 1997

The Mona Passage is the treacherous pass between the Dominican Republic and the island of Puerto Rico. A fast powerboat can head east on a straight course and be across in several hours. Sailing, however, takes two nights and a day. We left Samana at 6:00pm. Winds and switching currents made it difficult to hold a course. By heading northeast the first 24 hours we avoided the thunderstorms that blow off Puerto Rico every night and move out over the Mona Passage.

The United States Coast Guard maintains a vigilant patrol of the area for drug runners and illegal aliens sneaking into the U.S. through Puerto Rico. We were buzzed three times by two planes and a Coast Guard helicopter. Each one took a very close look at our boat. Our passage was not an enjoyable one. It was not horrible, but not pleasant either. At the end of the second day I heard the heart stopping words no sailor ever wants to hear.

"We're taking on water!" Ken yelled up to me from below.

"What do you mean? How much water? What happened?" I screeched from the helm where I strained to look down below. Water covered the cabin floor. I fought a feeling of dread that could have easily escalated into terror. *Stay calm. It's not time to panic, yet. Ken will take care of it. At least we know the U.S. Coast Guard is close by.*

"I don't know. The engine looks OK", Ken reported. "The bilge is not full."

Minutes stretched out like hours. My mind raced full speed ahead to an abandon ship scenario. I made a mental list of what we needed to grab if we had to get off the boat...*ship's papers, passport, water, flashlight, GPS, batteries, hand line and fishing lure, cash, knife....* "I think I found it!" Ken hollered. "It's the water pump for the deck wash down. It's cracked." He closed the seacock and stopped the incoming rush of water. "Don't worry, we're not sinking. But we do have a big mess."

I was very relieved, yet tired and angry. The cleanup got delegated to me. (Surprise, surprise) Adding to the mayhem, at some point, the coffee pot had flown off the stove in the rolling action and dumped coffee grounds onto rugs that were already soaked with salt water. *I am NOT having fun I don't want to be here!* With a lot of whining, I proceeded to clean up the worst of the mess inside the rolling, pitching boat. The rest could wait until we anchored. I was cranky from lack of sleep and uncomfortable from the unusual motion of the boat. Soon it would be dark again and the thought of another long, sleepless night was disheartening to me.

"I hate this!" I cried. "Why are we doing this?"

Ken tried to calm me down and cheer me up. "We're OK. Everything is fine. We'll be there in the morning. Don't be a wimp. Have a beer!" *I hate being called a wimp!*

I did get through another night with an hour or two of rest. After thirty-nine hours we had the anchor down in Boqueron on the south coast of Puerto Rico. Twelve hours of uninterrupted sleep did wonders for my outlook on cruising. I was happy again. I realized we were officially in the Caribbean Sea. We made it! The hard parts of the trip were behind us... I hoped.

Chapter 6
The Leeward & Windward Islands

May 26, 1997

Sunny, leisurely days in the Virgin Islands became a rewarding reprieve after hundreds of miles of persistent pushing to windward. Our daughter, Kassie joined us again in Puerto Rico after completing her freshman year of college and cruised with us for two weeks. The Spanish Virgin Islands, the U.S. and British Virgin Islands offered idyllic cruising grounds with turquoise water for snorkeling, snug coves for anchoring and easy sails between islands.

We cleared BVI Customs and Immigration on the island of Jost Van Dyke. The next order of business was an obligatory visit to Foxy's Beach Bar. We were lucky to find Foxy, himself, surrounded by a small crowd doing what he is famous for—singing silly songs and telling stories while his fans bought him beer and rum. In his Calypso story-telling style, Foxy incorporated our arrival into the song he happened to be singing.

Ken and I first visited Foxy's ten years earlier and enjoyed the funky little tiki bar on the beach. Apparently, thousands of other visitors loved it too, which prompted Foxy to expand in order to accommodate the ever-increasing crowds. This time there was a large covered dining area, beach volleyball nets and a boutique full of "Foxy's" souvenirs. The place was now a big business with big prices to match. I can't blame him for his savvy marketing moves but I preferred all the character of the original low-key beach bar.

The next morning we woke to the sound of goats bleating on the hillside and crowing roosters. Before pulling up the anchor we went back ashore for a loaf of freshly baked bread. A caramel colored cow stood tied at the end of the pier when we arrived. Ken has a soft spot in his heart for cows so he stepped close to have a few words with the brown-eyed bovine. Several men appeared, including Foxy and his dog, to take the cow down the dock to the waiting ferry boat.

How many men does it take to guide a cow down a pier? Three men pulled on the lead rope and horns. Two more pushed from behind while the dog nipped at the cow's heels. Bessie did *not* want to go! I happened to have my camera with me and shot pictures of the whole kooky ordeal. Foxy asked me to send him some photos because that was the last cow on Jost Van Dyke.

The scene turned into a real fiasco. The poor cow struggled, eyes white with terror, as three of her legs slipped between the boat and the pier. The local contingency heaved and pushed, the dog barked and cow pies mucked up the dock. At that point Ken was in the thick of things. From the boat he pulled on her horns and murmured positive suggestions into her ear. Finally, that poor cow was tied safely aboard the ferry. Ken was sure that it was his hypnosis skills that encouraged her for the last few steps over the gap and onto the boat.

I looked over the photos a few weeks later and decided it would be appropriate to include a calypso style poem with those pictures that I had promised to send to Foxy. Ken immediately jumped into creative action and wrote a song entitled "My Sweet Brown Cow—She Don't Want to Go". (Yes, we occasionally have a lot of extra time on our hands!) We never heard from Foxy about the piece so we'll never know if it was added to his repertoire.

June 16, 1997

From the British Virgin Islands we headed for St. Martin to join the 50th birthday celebration of a good friend and fellow cruiser. The eighty nautical miles of water between Virgin Gorda, BVI and St.Martin is called the Anagoda Passage—often referred to as the "Oh-My-Godda Passage". Heading to St.Martin our point of sail was close-haul, bashing and crashing right into the wind. Dumb. At 3:00am, midway across, we had enough and fell off the wind for a more comfortable beam reach toward the island of Saba. We were disappointed to miss the celebration but preferred not to beat ourselves up—not to mention our boat. After a rest at Saba in blustery winds we continued east to St. Kitts.

Once we were in the lee of St. Kitts my thoughts of giving up cruising vanished. The seas calmed and I focused on the tropical scene ashore. Kelly-green fields of sugar cane climbed up the slopes of a dormant volcano and merged with a tangle of jungley vegetation until the mountain peak dissolved into the clouds. For a couple of hours along the coastline, our sail was pure pleasure—one of those moments when the right amount of wind, from the right direction, filled our sails and pulled the boat along through the rippling water. I felt the warm breeze in my hair, the hot sun on my skin and tasted the salt on my lips. I heard the squawk of sea birds overhead and the splash of the water against the hull. It was so soothing that, at that moment, all was right with the world and there was no where else I would rather be.

We anchored in the harbor of Basseterre, the capital of St. Kitts and promptly reported to Customs and Immigration. Because we had a shotgun on board (which we were beginning to regret due to the hassle) the customs officer was required to escort us back to *Iniki* to "seal the weapon". He would not go in our dinghy so we took their 80-foot coast guard vessel. The vessel towered over *Iniki.* I held my breath as we came along side her. The driver was having difficulty due to wind and current so Ken insisted they put out more fenders to protect *Iniki's* hull. We had to jump from the coast guard boat down onto our deck as both boats rose and fell out of sync in the waves--not an easy thing to do. Surrounded by the navy boys in their fatigues it felt like some military boot camp training operation. The official wrapped and taped up our shotgun and ammunition, stamped official seals on it, then locked it in our lazerette (we kept the key—go figure!) Next came the boot camp challenge of climbing back up onboard the 80-foot vessel to return to the island. *All that effort for an overnight stay?* Reconsidering, we stayed on St. Kitts for two nights and toured Brimstone Hill Fortress, a sugar plantation and the batik factory on the island.

Already late June, hurricane season had begun. Ken kept a close watch on the tropical waves that typically developed out in the Atlantic about every three days. A tropical wave can become a tropical depression that can turn into a storm and then a hurricane. We had to keep sailing south to get out of the hurricane zone that runs from 35 degrees north (Norfolk, VA) to 12 degrees north (Grenada, BWI).

A batten worked itself out of our mainsail between St. Kitts and her sister island Nevis. Minor repairs were required before continuing, so we anchored off a pretty beach near the Four Seasons Resort. A monstrous full moon silently dominated the eastern night sky that evening. As it rose over the island, moonbeams crept down the mountainside and out over the water casting a soft, silvery glow on all the boats in the bay. *Another magical scene to commit to memory.*

At daybreak we set a course for Martinique, giving the rumbling island, Montserrat, a very wide berth. The volcano on Montserrat erupted a few days later spreading devastation over the island for months. We sailed south past Guadeloupe the following night. *Iniki* plunged ahead under a double-reefed main sail in total blackness with twenty-eight knots of wind and eight to twelve-foot seas on the beam. During my watch, I couldn't get comfortable in the cockpit. The boat heeled over so far in the strong wind that I had to stretch my legs in two different directions to brace myself. I double-checked my harness connection to the jack lines. My mood deteriorated rapidly when a wall of water crashed over the rail into the cockpit and drenched me.

"AAUGH!" I yelled in shock. *Iniki* was a very dry sailboat and we rarely took water over the side. The night was so black that I could not see the wave coming in time to duck out of the way. Another wave followed right behind the first. The cool water hit me again and ran down the back of my neck under my shirt.

"FUCK!" I screamed into the wind. Although it was not an active word in my vocabulary under normal circumstances, it definitely helped relieve my frustration at that moment. In fact, it felt so good to shout it, I proceeded to spew out every other swear word I could think of in one, long string of expletives. Unfortunately, the wild-woman act didn't dilute my uneasiness over the current sailing conditions. I woke Ken early for his shift. One look at my face and he knew I wasn't happy.

"What's the matter?" Ken asked.

"What's the matter?" I echoed with amazement. As the wind howled, the boat continued to buck and roll. "Waves are coming over the rail. I'm wet, miserable and I'm scared!" I said, enlightening him to what seemed obvious to me.

"*Iniki* loves this." Ken responded surprised that I wasn't having a ball. "She's made for conditions like this. She's handling just fine."

"But I don't feel safe." I whimpered and convinced him we should take a third reef in the main. Ken studied the chart and our position. We would have to sail another day and night to reach Martinique, Ken's planned destination.

"I don't see why we can't stop at one of these islands and take a break.", I continued.

Negotiations ensued between the Captain (Ken) and the Admiral (me). As a result, we tacked and set a course for the nearest island--Dominica. Dominica is "The Nature Island" and is less developed than the neighboring islands. It has two seasons: wet and wetter! Fruits, vegetables and flowering plants flourish in this lush and fertile environment.

There were three familiar sailboats already anchored in the bay by the town of Portsmouth when we arrived after sun-up. Before we even had our anchor down, one of our friends came over by dinghy to invite us to a get-together on their boat later in the afternoon.

From Dominica we day-sailed down-island stopping at Martinique, St. Lucia, St. Vincent, Bequia, Mustique, Mayreau, Palm Island, Union Island, Carriacou and Grenada. Each one had its own charm. I would have enjoyed staying longer in the Grenadines but we had to get south! No time to linger during hurricane season.

Local Boat, Mustique

Arriving in Grenada

When we arrived in St. George Harbor on Grenada, Ken and I heaved a sigh of relief to be safely at the magical latitude that insurance companies declare to be safe during hurricane season. But we still needed to keep moving. We had airline tickets to fly to the States for a family wedding from Trinidad, eighty miles farther south. The next day we sailed around to the south side of Grenada and prepared *Iniki* for the overnight passage. Ken calculated the trip to be about sixteen hours. In order to arrive at our destination during daylight hours, we left our anchorage in Prickley Bay, Grenada at sunset and set sail for Trinidad. The wind was nineteen knots right on the beam--fantastic! But currents were so strong, that we averaged only two to three knots of speed in the six to eight-foot seas—not fantastic. At that rate it would take forever to reach Trinidad. Frequent squalls showered us as we passed through the ITZ--inter-tropical convergence zone.

The following day, on my watch, I heard a loud "pop". Startled, I jumped and looked around to figure out what happened. One of the D-rings broke on the dinghy we were towing. Now it was attached to the towing bridle on only one side instead of two, and weaved wildly off our stern.

"Ken!" I yelled. "I need you on deck."

Quickly surveying the situation, Ken announced we would hove-to—a method of stopping the boat by back-winding the jib. Once the boat was stopped he could reconnect the towing bridle on the dinghy. First I needed to reel in the fishing line.

"Be sure not to get the treble hook caught on the dinghy", he warned.

Wouldn't you know it...as I reeled in the line, a wave hit the lure at the worst possible moment. The "dolphin delight" lure bounced right into the dinghy and stuck. *Great!* Ken pulled the dinghy along side the boat. In the process, he banged his knee hard in the unsteady cockpit. He yelled in pain as he quickly tied the dinghy painter around a winch. I was ready to fetch some ice for his knee when I glanced up and saw the dinghy drifting away from us.

"The dinghy is loose!" I shouted. "Hey, wait! It's still hooked on the fishing line." I watched Ken reel in the catch and hoped the hooks didn't puncture the inflatable. It was a tense situation but at the same time I saw the comic scenario. *This is really very funny but I dare not laugh now.* The good news/bad news episode lasted forty-five minutes. This was *not* one of those previously mentioned smooth sailing moments! Our easy sixteen-hour crossing became a tough twenty-two hours. Once the island of Trinidad was in sight, we could also see Venezuela. The South American continent was only eight miles from the Chagaramus peninsula on the northwest corner of Trinidad.

We tied up at the customs dock in Chagaramus, went through the required song and dance with the officials and then got a slip at Crews Inn Marina. The next morning Ken left the boat to find a newspaper. At the newsstand he met a Greek commercial shipping captain who was fishing through his pockets for the right coins to buy a paper as well. Ken gave him the coin he needed. The two recognized their similarities—same height and build and lack of hair. They could have been brothers. When Ken returned to *Iniki* he told me of his encounter with the Greek Captain. "We are invited to join him for dinner on his ship at 1:00pm today."

"What kind of ship? What do we wear? Should we take something?" I asked. I had visions of Aristotle Onassis and some fancy mega yacht.

Ken looked at me like I was nuts. "It's a commercial ship. He's delivering a load of soda ash. I don't know how big it is. The man just seemed like he was lonely for some company."

I rummaged through our provisions and pulled out a bottle of red wine and a jar of Greek olives—not much but a gesture anyway. A few hours later we walked down to the end of the marina, away from the pleasure boats, turned a corner by some warehouses to the commercial pier. Three freighters were tied up. One was rustier than the next.

"Which one is it?" I asked, looking over the three fine examples of deferred maintenance and realized how ridiculous it was to worry about how to dress for the occasion.

"It's that second one," Ken said, pointing to the middle ship.

A crew dressed in gray jumpsuits worked on deck. We stopped along side and Ken shouted up to one of the men. "Is the Captain on board?"

A man waved us aboard. I gingerly climbed the narrow rickety gangplank. We were led up some more stairs at the stern of the ship and into a small dining room. One table and several folding chairs filled the space. The tablecloth was stained and covered with crumbs from some previous meal. Greek music blared from an old radio sitting at the end of the table. Spiro, the Captain, was overjoyed that we came. He hugged Ken like a long lost friend and kissed my hand. When I gave him the olives and bottle of wine he clasped both his hands to his chest and exclaimed, "You're breaking my heart. Sit-sit!"

Shouting into the galley in his native tongue produced an instant response. The cook delivered three glasses and poured rum & cokes. Spiro sat down and launched into a long-winded summary of his troubles with the ship owner who won't send money to pay his men, problems with the local shipping agent in Trinidad, the importance of respect, and the importance of enjoying life. I had trouble understanding his heavy accent but it wasn't an issue because after the initial greeting full of charm and compliments, I was ignored. Spiro spoke to Ken. If I asked a question he responded to Ken. I, the woman, became invisible. I found that fascinating. I had fun testing my theory. Each time I interjected comments in the conversation it went unacknowledged. Ken knowingly gave me a wink. I hid my amusement and sat quietly and observed.

After a simple meal Ken was taken on a tour of the bridge. I tagged along. Ken was interested to learn that the Greek used the exact same GPS that we had on our sailboat. Before we left Spiro told Ken he was leaving at noon the following day headed for Guyana. So tonight he was going to "a very nice casino".

"You come here at 10:00pm. I have a driver to take us and bring us back to the ship. It's vip treatment all the way." (Spiro said "vip", not V.I.P.)

Ken thought it would be interesting. I knew I was in for another "seen but not heard" session, but I had no intention of letting Ken go without me. *Maybe there will be some live steel drum music or other entertainment there to enjoy.*

We returned to the ship at the designated time. The Captain proudly brought out a new bottle of Johnny Walker Blue Label and poured drinks for all. He gave a small toast, emptied his glass and gave the order; "Now we go."

The cab driver looked like Mike Tyson and the casino wasn't at all what I expected. It was a dark, clandestine place with a disguised second entrance past the front door. The operation had been there for years but only recently legal after changes in the gambling laws. Many of the patrons were Chinese. All the dealers knew Cap-ee-tan. They spoke to him with deference. ("vip treatment") An unattractive hooker stuffed into leather short-shorts, fishnet stockings and glittery, silver shoes attached herself to Cap-ee-tan's arm and oozed adoration that suggested even more vip treatment later.

The place gave me the creeps. Ken was learning how to play Caribbean poker so I played the slot machines and quickly lost 80 TT's (about $13.00) When the time came I was happy to leave. Ken and I climbed into the back seat of the small driven by Mike Tyson's twin. Miss Short-shorts sat on the Cap-ee-tan's lap and also returned to the ship. We said good night and quickly departed to go to our own boat. "Gee, Ken, you take me to the nicest places," I teased.

July 12, 1997

We left *Iniki* at Crews Inn Marina and flew back to the United States to attend my cousin's wedding in Colorado Springs. After the fun family reunion Ken and I flew on to Chicago to visit his family there. My annual mammogram revealed another small lump in the same location as the previous year. *Not again!* The doctors were very cooperative about squeezing me into their schedules for a biopsy. The lump was removed in an outpatient facility with local anesthetic. It was benign. *Must I go through this scare every year?*

    I couldn't wait to see family and friends after being away for twelve months. However, once back in the States I soon realized a change within myself. Over time I had disassociated myself from that old lifestyle. After our enjoyable visit with loved ones I was anxious to return to our sailboat and our life on the water.

Chapter 7
Trinidad to Venezuela

August 10, 1997

Sailboats from all over the world filled the harbors and boatyards around Port of Spain, Trinidad. I saw flags from France, Germany, Great Britain, Sweden, Norway, Denmark, Canada, South Africa, Australia, New Zealand, Panama, Brazil, Bahamas, USA and some flags I couldn't identify. Among cruisers Trinidad is known as the place to have "boat work" done. "Boat work" is a catchall for painting, varnishing, sail repair, mechanical maintenance and repair as well as interior refurbishing, such as new cushions or curtains. That industry has exploded in Trinidad in the last ten years and the experts (and there are many who do excellent work) can't keep up with the demand. So an assistant's friend or brother scoops up the excess work and may or may not be as skilled as they say they are. It was important to get referrals from a reputable boatyard and closely supervise the work.

Many sailors who arrived became involved in annual preparations and festivities of world-renowned Carnival and tried to convince us to stick around six more months to experience the party of parties preceding Lent. But huge, drunk, mud-slinging crowds were not at all enticing to me. Even though we enjoyed the blended culture, wonderful steel drum music and nature preserves, we felt like something was missing. It was clean, clear water. Flotsam and jetsam littered the muddy brown seawater around Port of Spain. Everything that flowed out the mouth of the mighty Orinoco River, just across the Gulf of Paria, washed up on Trinidad's western shore. Daily rain showers washed mud and trash off hillsides and carried it to the already-murky water. I would not even put my big toe in that water. Ken and I were anxious to move on to a place where we could swim, snorkel and fish again.

Bake & Shark Hut in Trinidad

August 30, 1997

We sailed to the island of Chacachacare, only five nautical miles from Chagaramus Peninsula, where we had been in Trinidad. The small island was once a leper colony. Long since deserted and overgrown, the island offers a quiet, pretty anchorage to boaters.

Heading west the next day we soon entered Venezuelan waters. The high, steep cliffs along the northern coastline of Venezuela blocked the wind, so we motored most of the way along the Paria Peninsula against strong currents. The smooth water was a brilliant green color. Thousands of transparent jellyfish pulsated just below the surface.

Venezuelan Coast

Approximately eighty miles long, the Paria Peninsula is extremely remote and accessible only by boat. We stopped for the night at Cabo San Francisco, one of the two suitable overnight anchorages along that stretch of the coast. The rest of the peninsula is exposed to weather, offering no shelter from the winds and seas. San Francisco Bay was stunning. Steep jungle-covered cliffs rose straight up to the clouds. The exotic sounds of howler monkeys and parrots echoed through the treetops. Coconut palms, mango trees, breadfruit and flowering plants lined the sand beach and a fresh-water stream emptied into the bay. It was a setting worthy of Swiss Family Robinson. As a kid I was fascinated with the jungle and watched all the Tarzan movies. So even though we never left our boat, I was thrilled to see such a beautiful, isolated place and listen to all the wild sounds.

Local fisherman stopped near the stream to fill containers with fresh water, wash clothes, eat, and rest before a night of fishing at sea. I loved the colorful paint jobs and creative names on their wooden boats, called "pineros". Ken admired their design and seaworthiness.

Before retiring for the night I stepped up on deck for a look around. My motive was partly for security but I also wanted to check out the night sky, since we were so far from city lights. The heavens glittered and twinkled with billions of stars.

I didn't want Ken to miss the incredible sight. "Hey, Ken! You've gotta come look at the sky." Then, I noticed the water. Bioluminescence and phosphorescence shimmered under the glassy surface. Clouds of light swirled with schools of fish. We saw the glow of a large fish (or shark?) as it cruised by our boat. The bay was teeming with life. In the morning we continued along the coast for a few hours to another beautiful bay. We spent the afternoon resting and prepared *Iniki* for an overnight sail to a small group of islands called Los Testigos (The Witnesses), about sixty nautical miles to the northwest. While we relaxed a small fishing boat approached with fish for sale. We had no local currency yet, so Ken offered four cold beers for three nice red snapper. It was a good trade and everyone was happy. We dined on fresh fish and rice as the last rays of sun danced off the face of the cliffs before sinking below the horizon.

That evening at 9:00 pm we hauled up the anchor. The wind blew eight to ten knots on our quarter with three-foot following seas. A favorable current provided an extra push on a very pleasant passage. Navigator Ken predicted a 9:00am arrival. After sailing all night we arrived at Testigo Grande at exactly 9:00 am and were escorted into the bay by four large dolphins swimming in our bow wake. A nice welcome!

As we anchored I was surprised at the difference from the lush mainland we left the night before. These three little islands that made up Los Testigos were arid and sparse and the crystal-blue water reminded us of the Bahamas. The friendly commandante at the Coast Guard Station stamped our papers and gave us permission to stay for three days. He seemed happy to talk to someone and practiced a few English words on us. It must be a lonely post for a young man. On the other hand, who could complain about an assignment in paradise?

Avoiding the ten other sailboats clustered off the largest beach, we found our own secluded cove to anchor and snorkeled most of the afternoon. Miniature white butterflies flitted erratically through the air like snowflakes in the wind. Shrubs vibrated with white, fluttering wings. Ken thought it was a migration but they didn't seem to be going in any particular direction. Maybe that island *was* their destination.

Late in the afternoon a large pinero with 10 to12 fisherman aboard chugged in and anchored near us. Since they stared at us as they went by, we waved. They waved back and went about their chores. Soon a gorgeous sunset was in progress. Ken and I sat in the cockpit and watched, sipping sundowners, as the sky turned fluorescent shades of red, orange and purple. We marveled at the fact that we were *really* in Venezuela, on our *own* boat!

"Can you believe it? We sailed this sailboat from Chicago, 3000 miles to South America!"

"We said we were gonna do it and we did it," Ken said.

Feeling quite pleased with ourselves, we continued to pat each other on the back and contemplated our accomplishment. We had extricated ourselves from all those material attachments and creature comforts on land, whittled down our "stuff" to the bare necessities that would fit on a 34-foot-long, 11-foot-wide sailing vessel, and set out in slow motion to see what we could see. We had adjusted quite well to the new lifestyle-- and we were still talking to each other!

No doubt the rum enhanced our euphoric mood. I decided we needed some music to accompany the moment, so I turned on a CD of traditional Venezuelan folk songs on guitar and quatro. Nearby the fishermen were busy with boat chores.

"Turn it up so the fishermen can hear," Ken suggested.

When the men on the colorful pinero heard the music, they smiled and gestured approval. Thirty minutes passed. The light was nearly gone when one of the brown, leather- skinned fishermen rowed over to us in a small wooden dinghy. He handed us a bucket of tiny fish, all about six to eight inches long. He spoke no English. In Spanish he said his name was Fred. He was thin and wore torn sweatpants with the Chicago Bulls logo on a leg.

At first we thought Fred was selling the fish, but he made it clear that he wanted no money. The fish was a "regalo"--a gift from his captain to thank us for the "beautiful symphony". He said they liked the music very much. *How sweet!* The fish were white grunts and normally I wouldn't bother eating fish that small. But how could we say no to such a nice gesture?

· "Muchas gracias por los pescados," I said in my poor Spanish. I put the fish in a bowl and passed back the bucket. Fred's hand motions were wonderful as he described how to scale and fry the fish. Then he kissed his fingertips like a French chef's declaration of a culinary delight and finished with the Venezuelan finger snap, a gestured exclamation point used often by Venezuelan men.

Ken wanted to give a gift in return. He dug out some shelled pecans from our provisions and gave the bag to Fred to share with the others. I scored, seasoned and fried the fish as instructed. They tasted great but it wasn't enough food for my husband. He needed a large bowl of popcorn to supplement the meal.

In order to better hear the music the fishermen let out more anchor line to get closer and closer to our boat. Before long they were within spitting distance. In the dark our new friends sat on the rail of their pinero, with one small light, and munched pecans while they listened to Placido Domingo's "My Latin Soul" and Julio Iglesias' "Tango". At 9:00 pm it was time for them to go to work. The Venezuelans pulled up their anchor and slowly disappeared into the darkness.

I listened to the rhythmic sound of their engine as they departed and marveled at what had transpired. We were strangers—the Venezuelan fishermen and the American travelers. Yet each of us reached out to the other, ignoring barriers of language and profession and economic class. That magical evening we were all "marineros" living on the sea. We touched each other's lives. The experience nudged me further down my pathway of change.

Venezuelan Fishing Boat

Sunset Venezuela

September 8, 1997

The island of Margarita is a very popular vacation destination for Venezuelans and Europeans, offering beautiful beaches and duty-free shops with everything imaginable. Alejandro, our friend from Caracas, flew over to join us for two days to celebrate Ken's 52nd birthday. The three of us spent the afternoon at the nicest public beach on the island--Playa El Agua. Fifty open-air restaurants lined the waterfront. Alejandro introduced me to a very cool and refreshing drink called a Kaiperina, made with Cachasa from Brazil, crushed limes, sugar and water. After two drinks I found a lounge chair and felt nearly comatose. The two men walked up and down the beach, feasting their eyes on all the beautiful women in dental- floss swimsuits.

From Margarita Ken and I sailed south toward the mainland and into Mochima National Park. Underway I noticed some splashing and churning water off our port side about a mile away. I thought the splashes were from a big school of fish. Hoping to catch dinner, I turned the boat and headed toward the erupting water. Curious to find out what was causing the commotion, I grabbed the binoculars. Suddenly, I saw dolphins everywhere. We were soon surrounded by *thousands* of leaping dolphins! The pod covered a square mile area—layer upon layer. They surfaced and jumped in sync, six at a time, then swiftly shifted position with another bunch. They swam in the bow wake, along side, behind, and under the keel. I hung out over the bow and shrieked with delight as I listened to their high-pitched calls and watched them zigzag with incredible speed. Completely mesmerized, I could not tear myself away to go for my camera. We stayed with dolphins--or they stayed with us--for at least forty-five minutes. Still on my dolphin high I retrieved my Audubon fish book and identified them as common dolphins. They were smaller that the more familiar bottlenose dolphins and had cream-colored sides and bellies. Noted for gathering in huge groups, they were probably feasting on the sardines that are abundant in Venezuelan waters. Three more times that afternoon groups of ten to twenty dolphins rode our bow wake, then disappeared as suddenly as they had arrived.

Mochima National Park is believed to be a sunken valley cutting into the mainland, with several fingers off the main bay to explore. We cruised into one of those long, narrow fingers, where it felt like we were in a mountain lake. Low red mountains covered with scrubby shrubs and cactus surrounded us. Farther inland, as the elevation increased, so did the vegetation and foliage.

Flocks of green parrots congregated in the desert shrubs. If you have been to the desert and seen the late-afternoon light play on the rocks, bringing out all the subtle earth tones of yellow ochre, burnt sienna, raw umber, then you can imagine how lovely it was in Mochima. The water was smooth as glass, creating a perfect reflection of our mast and shrouds. That evening a full moon appeared from behind the mountains, making a late-night skinny dip irresistible.

We worked our way to Puerto La Cruz on the mainland of Venezuela, where we got a slip at the posh Mare Mare Resort and Marina. For $15 a day we had free water, a phone line, a huge swimming pool, a health club and fresh towels daily. It was a great base from which to explore the nearby islands. Our plan was to spend the remainder of the 1997 hurricane season there. We bought a tiny used Mini Cord car. It looked like a toy but was perfect to get around town for the three months we were there. We planned to sell it again before we moved on, although it was fiberglass, green and so small it could nearly fit on the bow deck of *Iniki*!

Chapter 8
Puerto La Cruz to Bonaire

September 17, 1997

Mare Mare Marina and Resort, located in Puerto La Cruz, Venezuela, was a safe, secure place to spend the last three months of hurricane season. We often rode in our dinghy from the marina through an intricate canal system lined with large, beautiful homes, to a nice shopping mall to see American movies with Spanish subtitles. If there were no posters outside the theater to provide a clue as to what was showing, it was difficult know what we were paying to see because of the strange title translations. For example, "El Complot" turned out to be "Conspiracy Theory" with Mel Gibson.

In October the heat was nearly unbearable. Ken bought a used air conditioner that fit over our salon hatch. Then, of course, we had to close up the companionway and all the portholes that made our small living area like a dark, underground cave. I hated it. When everything was open, the light and quick access to the outside made a huge difference to me psychologically.

"I don't get it. We left the cold weather for warmer climates, yet you have the air conditioner so cold that I have to wear long pants and long sleeves in here. That's crazy!" I complained.

We were so "plugged in" to land with the A/C, phone line and internet access right on the boat that our weekend sails to the offshore islands came to an end. *Iniki* sat at the dock growing algae and other life forms and disintegrating zincs with record speed.

We took advantage of the dry weather to work on the boat. We stripped the teak and applied numerous coats of Cetol with the help of Oscar, a young man who had worked on other boats in the marina. Ken demonstrated exactly how he wanted each step of the job done and he supervised his helper very closely. Oscar had never worked with Cetol before but he learned fast and worked hard. He spoke only a little English. Ken practiced his limited Spanish with Oscar and worked on increasing his own vocabulary. In order to describe the varnishing process to his helper, Ken looked up the Spanish words for "dust", "smooth" and "brush" in our Spanish/English dictionary. Occasionally, the transition from reading a word to pronouncing it correctly was a struggle with comical results. All day while the two of them worked, Ken repeated the phrase "dust is my enemy" to explain the need to carefully wipe away dust after sanding the wood between coats of varnish. The literal translation that Ken came up with himself was, "Me enemigo es polvo." But he mispronounced the last word-- the key word--so it sounded more like, "Me enemigo es pulpo." Oscar looked puzzled the first few times he heard Ken say this. He struggled to comprehend, but never laughed or showed any disrespect. One weekend while the project was still underway, our friend from Caracas drove to Puerto La Cruz to visit us again. When Alejandro came aboard *Iniki*, Ken repeated his phrase of the month, "Me enemigo es pulpo".

Alejandro was also puzzled and asked, "Why do you say that?"

In English Ken explained about varnish and dust.

"So what does octopus have to do with it? You are saying, 'My enemy is octopus!'"

Ken roared with laughter. "No wonder Oscar looked at me like I was crazy."

Now Oscar saw that it was safe to join in the joke and from then on, greeted Ken each morning by saying in English, "My enemy is octopus!"

We kept practicing our Spanish and learned new words. Everywhere we went our bumbling attempts were received with patience, gentle corrections and appreciation for the effort. Even so, I was embarrassed that I had not mastered a second language when so many people we met from around the world could speak 2, 3 or 4 languages fluently.

November 15, 1997

Hurricane season was nearly over and cruisers began to leave Puerto La Cruz daily. The majority headed back north to the Virgin Islands. Many went to Trinidad for carnival and some sailed west. Ken and I were also itching to move on. We sold our portable air conditioner to a boater who was staying in Puerto La Cruz and with the help of our good friend in Caracas we sold our mini cord car for what we paid for it. Next, we had *Iniki* hauled out of the water and repainted the bottom.

Iniki hauled out for fresh bottom paint, Venezuela

Venezuelan Customs and Immigration required three days to process our clearance papers for departure. While we waited we loaded up the boat with canned goods, fresh vegetables, snacks, soda, Polar beer, oil filters, spark plugs and fishing lures. We would be spending the next few weeks in some remote islands where nothing was available except the seafood we could catch ourselves.

December 11, 1997

The time came to say "hasta la vista" to our friends at Mare Mare Marina. Sailing six miles across the bay, we tacked around several humongous oil tankers that were anchored outside the port. Rounding Isla Borracha (The Drunk Woman) we dropped the hook for the night in a tight anchorage under a steep cliff with howling winds. At dusk, holes in the cliffs erupted with a squeaking, fluttering mass of bats. Like a scene from a horror movie the bats swooped around us, skimmed over the water, cut left then right as they zeroed in on the evening insects.

"Put on the screens! Cover the companionway!" my brave husband yelled as he raced below for cover. Safely below, I turned on the stereo so I wouldn't hear those creepy bat sounds! In the early morning darkness we pulled up the anchor to sail fifty nautical miles northwest to the island, La Tortuga (The Turtle). As we adjusted the sails I heard dolphins and scanned the black water until I spotted them. The ten dolphins that raced along side our bow appeared to be red and green in the glow of our navigation light.

Throughout the day Ken and I bumbled around on deck like a couple of landlubbers. After three months tied to a dock we lost our sea legs and I acquired a fresh collection of bruises. The sail to La Tortuga was a fast—eight hours instead of the predicted ten. La Tortuga lies 10 degrees 58 minutes north and 65 degrees 20 minutes west. It is a low, flat island that is difficult to spot until you are within two or three miles of it. The long beaches, blinding in the intense sunlight, appeared snowy white next to the cerulean blue water. I had a recurring problem whenever we approached the beach by dinghy. As we got close, Ken tilted up the outboard motor and I hopped out in knee-deep water to pull the dinghy up on shore. But, time after time, I was fooled by the clarity of the water. What looked like knee-deep water was really up to my chin!

The island was sparse with nothing but a lighthouse, a fisherman's camp, a runway and perfect beaches. On the weekend small planes flew over from the mainland. Their passengers spent the afternoon on the beach under striped umbrellas with coolers and toys then flew back to Caracas before sundown.

Lobsters were in season again and the local fishermen had plenty. We went ashore to their camp and Ken spoke "Spanglish", muttering a few words like "buenos dias" and "langosta?" (lobster?) and "mi Espanol es malo" (My Spanish is bad). I stood by smiling and offered a few Spanish verbs when necessary. The fisherman knew what we wanted and showed us the big holding pens where they kept the lobsters alive in the water. We picked out our dinner and paid them by weight. If no scale was available, they guessed the weight. Sometimes we got an extra lobster in exchange for a small $1.00 bottle of rum but they were mainly interested in cash.

Eighty-five nautical miles from La Tortuga was Los Roques (The Rocks). Los Roques is a protected Venezuelan National Park. It is an archipelago of about forty islands around a shallow lagoon covering an area approximately fourteen miles by twenty-five miles. Several islands are restricted to protect sea turtles, conch and bird nesting areas. But many others offer secluded anchorages to explore within easy sailing distances.

Our overnight sail from La Tortuga to Los Roques was comfortable and pleasant—going *with* the winds and currents for a change. It was a clear, starry night with 16-18 knots of wind abaft the beam and five-foot seas. We arrived sooner that we expected so we hove to for an hour. Ken thought it wise to wait for the sun to get higher, for better water visibility, before we tackled the tricky entrance through the reef. We sailed through the reef an hour later. The sun shimmered on the surface of the calm, protected water that looked like flowing ribbons of brilliant green and blue. It was easy see the sand bars and coral heads we needed to avoid.

Our first stop was the main island of Gran Roque to check into the park. The process required visits to four different authorities in the proper order—Navy, Coast Guard, Customs and Immigration—and took four hours.

December 18, 1997

The little town of Gran Roque was all decorated for Christmas. There were no cars on the island so the roads and paths were all sand. Strings of Christmas lights were strung between the buildings across the main thoroughfare. Cute, brightly painted guesthouses, small restaurants welcomed the visitors who arrived by boat or by small plane. It took no time at all to see the whole town on foot and we were soon back aboard our boat in search of a more secluded anchorage away from all the tourists.

Off the island of Sarqui, which was a low, treeless island with a long, powdery beach and surrounded by a coral reef, we anchored in sand next to a large dark patch, which we assumed to be grass. A bit later we noticed that the large dark spot moved a few feet. We grabbed our masks and fins and jumped in the water to investigate. The grass patch was actually a thick school of finger-sized fish— millions of them, all following an unknown leader in a circular rotation. The safety-in-numbers clump, however, only provided a convenient target for the pelicans that lined up overhead like a precision bomber team. In turn, one after the other, they rolled and dove into the school of fish, gulped down their catch, took off and lined up to dive again.

December 24, 1997

The winds steadily increased during that week we cruised through the park. I thought it would be nice to go back to Gran Roque to attend Christmas Eve service in the tiny chapel we saw but that island was twenty miles east of us. It would mean sailing into 25-30 knots of wind and fighting the current as well. The captain said it wasn't a smart plan. Although I was disappointed, I knew he was right. By that time we were in a beautiful little lagoon at the eastern end of Carenero. It was the most protected anchorage in the park so we stayed where we were.

That day we swam, snorkeled and read on the beach. We visited a fisherman's camp to buy some lobsters for Christmas dinner. We paid the equivalent of about $14.00 for three large lobsters. One of the small men flexed his muscles and pointed to Ken to acknowledge he was a big, strong guy. "Americano?" he asked.

"No, yo soy Maricucho!" (No, I am from Maricaibo) We're still not sure why the locals think that is so funny. Apparently, the people from the second largest city in Venezuela are somehow recognizable and different from the rest of the Venezuelans. But Ken, the obvious gringo, always got a big laugh and instant rapport when he said that.

I chilled a bottle of champagne I saved for the occasion and steamed the lobster tails for dinner. I hung a few decorations around the inside of the boat, and listened to Christmas Carols in an effort to fight off the blues. I love Christmas time with all its traditions. I love the baking and entertaining that add to the festivities. But it is people that really make it special. We were far away from family and friends and I was feeling lonely. Our isolation forced me to focus on the true meaning of Christmas without all the commercial distractions. I shared that celebration with my true love in a sunny island paradise. How could I ask for more than that? Christmas day in Los Roques was 78 degrees and sunny with 20 knots of wind out of the East. We had fun sending emails back and forth to family throughout the day. It was almost like being with them.

December 27, 1997

We left Los Roques at dawn and sailed west about forty miles to Aves de Barlovento, the first of two little archipelagos known as Las Aves (The Birds). *Iniki* raced ahead of the blustery winds and rode the large following seas like a roller coaster. The sight of the towering waves rising up behind us made me very nervous so I went below to avoid looking at them. Maybe I could go to sleep for a couple hours to pass the time.

A lighthouse stood at the end of Barlovento. Riding in on ten-foot waves we rounded the end of the island, zigzagged around reefs and coral heads in order to anchor behind the mangroves. As one might guess from the name of the islands, sea birds were everywhere—roosting in the trees, flying, diving and shrieking. The red-footed boobies were curious and flew close to our boat and spinning wind generator. At sunset long lines of birds returned from the sea for the night.

Las Aves Fisherman's Camp

The next morning we moved to an "ideal" anchorage recommended in our guidebook. It was only a mile away. However, the spot was not at all ideal in thirty knots of wind. The calm summer months are the best times to visit Las Aves, not December. *I just want to get to Bonaire and get out of these high winds!* We agreed to sail another twelve miles to the western islands of Las Aves. But first Ken thought is would be better to put the dinghy up on the bow. It was too hard to tow in the following seas. The rolling swells made the task of hoisting the dinghy more difficult than usual. In the middle of the process the anchor chain slipped, paying out anchor rode. I hustled back to the helm to put the boat in forward while Ken cleated the line.

With that problem taken care of we turned our attention back hoisting the dinghy up on the deck. I was nearly pushed overboard when a gust of wind caught the inflatable and backed me against the lifeline. Once it was tied down I went below and plopped down on the settee, feeling wind-whipped and frazzled.

Ken followed me down and cheerfully asks, "What's for lunch?"

Give me a break while I collect my wits. Didn't we just have breakfast? Heaven forbid we should skip a meal!

I fixed a quick lunch of tuna salad, cheese and crackers before we set sail again. The sky was bright blue without a cloud in the view. The winds remained a constant thirty to thirty-five knots all afternoon. The sight of the twelve to fifteen foot, breaking waves behind us still scared me. I wedged myself in the corner of the cockpit and hung on. Ken watched with delight as our speed registered on our hand held GPS. With jib sail only, *Iniki* was doing hull speed -- 7.6 knots. "This is great!" Ken grinned.

When I saw how well *Iniki* rode the seas and noted the man's joy, I relaxed a bit and decided we were OK. In less than two hours we turned to round the tip of the island and headed straight into the wind. When we passed by the edge of the reef we caught a nice yellow tail snapper. As soon as Ken hauled in the fish he tossed the line back out. It was time to furl in the reefed jib as we turned into the wind. When I released the jib sheet, the wind pulled the line so hard that my finger got caught and squashed on the cleat. At the same time another fish hit out lure. This time it was a barracuda. *Do we really need jaws full of teeth flopping around in the cockpit at this moment? It seems like we hook fish at the most chaotic times...not when we are ready and watching.* I steered the boat away from the reef until Ken could return to the helm.

My finger throbbed. I grabbed some ice to reduce the swelling then went to the bow to direct Ken through the coral hazards. Salty spray whipped off the choppy surface and soaked me for 3 long miles until we finally found some shelter behind some mangroves. *What a day! I need rum!* Ken administered liquid medication with a twist of lime to ease my pain and sooth my nerves. I did not relish the idea of facing another day like today but we had one more leg to reach Bonaire. *Let's just get there! Then we can relax in one place for a while.*

December 29, 1997

We left Las Aves after checking the weather fax at 9:00am. A Venezuelan Coast Guard helicopter circled us three times as we departed. It hovered and I could see a guy looking at us through binoculars. I waved. Half way to Bonaire we saw a ship on the horizon. We kept an eye on it as is got closer and closer.

"It looks like a military ship", Ken observed. "And it's heading straight for us!" Soon we heard a call over the VHF radio on channel 16. The voice spoke Spanish but we understood it was a call to the sailboat off the ship's bow. *That's us!* Ken responded in English--this was no time for bad Spanish and mispronunciation. In heavily accented English, the Venezuelan Navy radioman asked if we had an emergency.

"No" Ken responded. "No emergency. We are on our way to Bonaire."

"What is your course and speed?" they wanted to know.

"Course is 90 degrees. Speed is 5.5 knots", said Ken.

By this time the ship slowed behind us and came to a stop. We kept on sailing and there was no further contact. Thank goodness they didn't insist on boarding our boat in those rough seas.

The afternoon was hazy so we didn't spot Bonaire until we were just a few miles out. The first thing we saw through our binoculars was not a lighthouse but a high tech windmill! We should not have been surprised since the island is part of the Netherlands Antilles and Bonaire is the "B" in the "ABC Islands". Curacao and Aruba are the other two in the group.

We sailed around the Southern tip of Bonaire past salt flats and rows of abandoned concrete slave huts. *Were these actually living quarters for human beings?* Sailing North along the Western coastline we arrived at the only permissible anchorage area off the town of Kralendijk.

Finding an available mooring can we attached two bow lines. I immediately popped a cold can of beer to celebrate. I was ecstatic to be there! I felt as though I was falling apart emotionally over the last four days. The difficult sailing conditions and the remote isolation fueled my unhappy loneliness. I needed a dose of civilization and some interaction with other people. I wanted to stay for a couple months.

Our first impression of the cute town was that it was organized and clean, clean, clean! The people were warm and friendly. Our check-in with customs was a snap. Instead of ten stops with stacks of paperwork and stamps, we were greeted with: "Hi! Welcome to Bonaire. Stay as long as you like." The only rules had to do with protecting the reefs and Marine Park, their national treasure. The locals speak Dutch, English, Spanish, and Papiamentu, which is a combination of all of those languages with a little Portuguese, African and Arawak mixed in.

We arrived in time to celebrate the New Year, which we did in traditional Dutch fashion. We ate dinner and partied in De Tuin, a cute Dutch garden eatery with a crowd mostly from Amsterdam. Months slipped by in the beginning of 1998 as we enjoyed our free mooring. I was in no hurry to move on. We joined the wonderful health club/spa at Harbor Village Marina and worked out several days a week. We snorkeled and worked on the boat. The cruisers got together every week at a waterfront restaurant and we became friends with many local business owners on the island.

Bonaire

New Year's Eve on Bonaire 12-31-1997

Windward Shore on Bonaire

Bonaire's Interior

July 22, 1998

The sailboat was safe and secured in Harbor Village Marina when Ken and I
flew back to the United States for a family gathering to help my parents celebrate

their fiftieth wedding anniversary. Afterwards, our 12-year-old grandson, Jacob, flew back to Bonaire with us to spend a month on *Iniki*. Jake loves the water and, in no time, he was swimming among the fish and coral as if he had gills. Ken sparked his interest with spear-fishing stories and hoped to teach him how to use a Hawaiian sling—a long stick with a spear at one end and a stretchy rubber tubing at the other. We made plans to take Jake back to Las Aves for a couple weeks to fish and hunt lobsters. Since we didn't have a chance to really enjoy the area the previous December when the winds howled, we were anxious to return under the gentler summer winds.

Grandson, Jake learns to drive the dinghy

Chapter 9
Las Aves, Venezuela

August 3, 1998

Grandson, Jake, had a million questions about our planned sailing adventure to Las Aves. Ken went over the charts with him, explained time, speed and distance calculations, and GPS waypoints. Meanwhile, I made lists and provisioned the boat for the next month. We anticipated eating a lot of fresh fish and lobster so I focused on stowing fresh vegetables, eggs, rice, noodles, dry juice mix and plenty of snacks and goodies to keep a growing boy happy. Jake would have to settle for Pringles in those easy to store cans instead of his favorite, Doritos. The bags took up too much space. There are tough sacrifices to be made for so much fun!

Las Aves was forty-five nautical miles east of Bonaire, which required motor-sailing directly into the wind. Following the advice of other cruisers who regularly go back and forth, we left our mooring at 3:00am, when the winds are generally lighter. Once we sailed around the southern tip of Bonaire and out of the protection of the island we got a true reading of the wind and seas. The wind was still blowing 20-25 knots—too strong to head straight into it. Ken had prepared a backup plan in the event that the winds did not die down. So, switching to plan B, we continued on our southern course for the Venezuelan mainland, approximately ninety miles away--about the equivalent of sailing across Lake Michigan. We had a pleasant beam reach the whole way.

Jake woke up about 4:00 am, snapped on his safety harness and joined Ken and me in the cockpit. It was a moonless, black night. At first he chatted happily, in awe of the millions of stars blinking overhead. Suddenly, he looked around and noticed that we were out of sight of land. He got very quiet and worried. Soon he was curled up in the corner of the cockpit feeling seasick. He didn't move, other than to throw up, for the next 13 hours. *Poor kid!* The next afternoon about 5:00 pm, we arrived at Cayo Sal (Salt Key) near Chichrivichi. We anchored off a pretty beach full of coconut palms.

"Jake, you'll feel much better as soon as you jump in the water for a swim." I promised. Sure enough, the water revived him. His color returned and he was soon smiling and laughing again.

"So, Jacob, how did you like the 14-hour passage?" Ken asked.

Jake smiled and without hesitation replied, "It was cool!"

We stayed in that spot for two days, exploring and swimming and allowing our young crew to fully recover. His confidence returned after several successful day sails where he felt just fine. We explored Golfo de Cuare, a big shallow saltwater lake. The area is a wildlife refuge and part of Morrocoy National Park. One side of the gulf is lined with mangroves while the other side is a wall of limestone over two hundred feet high. The pockmarked cliffs have been eroded by winds and rain over the centuries creating many caves and caverns. We entered a cave that was presumably used as burial grounds by the Caquetios Indians, as far back as 3400 BC. *The first sign of bats and I'm out of here.* The Indian drawings on the inside walls were surprisingly well preserved.

We found another secluded grotto. Little statues of various saints and virgins were set in the holes in the rock cliff. Hundreds of candles, prayer cards, hats, rosaries and money were all left in the natural rock crevices because the grotto was believed to be a pool of healing, holy water.

At another anchorage in Morrocoy, we had fun driving our dinghy through narrow water passageways twisting and turning through the mangroves in the National Park. Thousands of birds nest there--frigates, herons, stilts, cormorants, terns, hawks, egrets and ibis. The most spectacular of all was the scarlet ibis. These crimson birds flew across the sky in long lines, like splashes of bright, red paint vibrating against a bright blue canvas.

The best anchorage in the park was Boca Seca (dry mouth), a spot between two islands protected behind a reef. There we got the benefit of the calm water as well as the nice sea breeze to keep away the mosquitoes and "no-see-ums", which can be dreadful near mangroves. When we arrived in Boca Seca, two other sailboats were already anchored. The homeport lettered on both boats was Maracaibo, Venezuela's second largest city after Caracas. Maracaibo is the oil capital of the country. I counted six teenagers between the two boats and when they saw Jake on board *Iniki*, they immediately came over in their dinghy. The kids didn't speak much English but they invited Jake to go snorkeling with them. When I translated for him, our grandson didn't even hesitate at the language handicap. He grabbed his mask and fins and off they all went.

Another one of our friends from Caracas drove to the park to visit us on the weekend. Juancho has a weekend condo nearby and keeps a powerboat in one of the marinas in Morrocoy. To Jake's delight, Juancho drove us around the islands in his "go-fast-boat". Then, much to *my* delight, I was able to use their washer and dryer in their condo to do our laundry. We stopped at a panaderia (bakery) in the little town of Tucacas and bought a bag of empanadas to eat. Empanadas are pastries filled with meat, cheese or fish and they are delicious!

When I finished folding our clean clothes, Juancho took us by boat to the popular island, Cayo Sombrero. Nearly one hundred other speedboats were already lined up along the beach for the afternoon. We swam and walked the beach until the boys started to think about food once again. Juancho made a call on his VHF radio. Fifteen minutes later, a large woman named Lillyana arrived with a man and boy in a small Pinero. She had several coolers in the boat from which she served plates of wonderful seafood. My mouth waters just from the memory of it. First, the woman pulled out a conch, sliced it thin and poured olive oil and fresh lime juice over it. The next plate was full of cold, cooked shrimp with sliced avocado and cocktail sauce. Out of another warmed container she scooped seafood paella onto a plate. There was a kind of cold soup that translates, "back to life", that was a combination of oysters, clams, squid, and octopus in a very spicy hot sauce. It is the Venezuelan cure for a hangover and also is supposed to be good for the libido. I tasted it but could barely get it down--definitely an acquired taste. Cold lobster, fish and octopus were also available from the floating gourmet. After serving our group, the man and boy cast off their lines and the threesome moved on to serve another boat.

The weekend crowds disappeared Sunday evening and we had the park to ourselves during the next week.

August 15, 1998

Jake had been aboard *Iniki* for over three weeks and was now breathing, eating and sweating sea salt and asking for more. With skin browned under the Caribbean sun and a bandana on his head, pirate style, he looked right at home on the sea. He learned knot tying. He knew how to whip lines and work the radio. He began to understand navigation, was an all round deck-swabber and stainless steel polisher. He helped his "Papa" change the oil in the diesel and even helped to rebuild the head. I think I saw him walk a little taller with pride in his new accomplishments and growing self-confidence.

We sailed along the mainland for six hours and arrived at Puerto Cabello, an official port of entry for the country. It is also the base for the Venezuelan Navy. We went directly to the Port Captain's dock to check in. There was no available dock space so we were instructed to raft off one of the pilot boats. Ken and Jake climbed over three ships to get to the pier and went off to find the customs office. They soon returned with a serious looking customs official dressed in a crisply pressed uniform, polished brass and spit-shined shoes. We invited him to come below to do the required paperwork at our salon table out of the blazing, hot sun. I offered him something to drink. The first can of Coca-cola I pulled out of the refrigerator was frozen so I set it aside while I dug around for another one. Meanwhile, Jake grabbed the frozen can and opened it. Bad move! Coke shot out of the can like a geyser--sending spray all over the cabin, the ship's papers and the officer. I groaned and reached for some paper towels. Ken apologized over and over and Jake wanted to slither under the rug and disappear. Fortunately for us, Senor Customs Official had a sense of humor. "Refrescante!" (Refreshing!), he said as he wiped off his face, arms and uniform. "No problema, Chico" (no problem, boy).

We were still red-faced when he informed us that our next required visit was to the immigration office. Since we were on a Navy Base, he told us, long pants were required. No shorts and no T-shirts. Once he left our boat we all changed into proper attire then climbed over the three ships and jumped down onto the pier. The three of us squeezed into the tiny air-conditioned immigration office for some more paperwork and purple stamps in our passports. When the man looked at Jake's passport he noticed his birthday was only three days away. The Venezuelan wished him a happy birthday and shook his hand.

We moved *Iniki* to the Puerto Cabello Yachting Club. After securing the boat in a slip Ken, Jake and I set off on foot to look around the little town. When we found the supermarket I told Jake he could pick out whatever he wanted to eat for his 12th birthday. He picked out chocolate chip muffins and milk for breakfast and hot dogs, Cheetos and a tin of gourmet Italian cookies for his special dinner. He thought he was in heaven with that stash!

The next morning was Saturday. The guys went off to find a marine store while I walked in the opposite direction to find the farmer's market. I found it a few blocks away and had fun wandering through the long aisles stacked high with fruits and vegetables. Other rickety stands were jammed with knock-off Tommy Hilfiger clothes, watches, sunglasses, junky plastic toys, American baseball caps, kitchen gadgets and kid's clothes. Children played under the tables and ran through the crowds.

Spanish words swirled around me at lightning speed as shoppers and venders made deals. I found some dish sponges and asked the vendor, "Cuanto por dos?" (How much for two?) Around the corner at another stand I bought some onions, avocadoes, carrots and tomatoes and put them into my backpack.

It must have been uncommon for an outsider to be shopping where the locals go. I was stared at like I had a flashing neon sign on my forehead announcing: GRINGA! It made me think about what I was doing. *Here I am, strolling by myself through this open market in a tiny, coastal town in South America, where no one speaks English. I am speaking Spanish, understanding the response and buying whatnots for the boat with Venezuelan Bolivars--and I feel comfortable doing it. Amazing!* Of course, I took precautions before wandering through the crowds on my own. I wore no jewelry, held on tightly to my backpack and kept my eyes open. But, on another level, I wanted to make a mental note of the "moment" and remember every detail of the not-so-ordinary shopping excursion. We had so many "moments" to remember on our travels and I wanted to highlight them with all of my senses to commit them to memory. *Some day I'm going to look back on this and marvel.*

We stayed at the marina in Puerto Cabello a day longer than we intended because *Iniki's* engine wouldn't start. Ken methodically checked all the wires, connections and batteries and cleaned all the battery terminal posts. Finally he discovered a corroded fuse connection on the alternator and installed a new fuse socket. When he connected the socket the engine still wouldn't start. Further examination found another connection had somehow been knocked off the starter solenoid. Reaching the solenoid required the unnatural physical contortions of a

Lilliputian. Ken just couldn't get his arms through to connect it. Jake gave it a go and almost succeeded but in the end, it took a woman to save the day. I wrestled blindly with the wire and after a struggle with grease and scrapes up to my elbows I managed to get it hooked up. We all held our breath as I turned the key. *Yes!* We love the sound of that purring diesel engine.

Jane the Mechanic

In the morning we sailed six miles to Isla Larga to stage ourselves for our passage north to Las Aves. The island turned out to be a delightful spot so we stayed on an extra day to celebrate our grandson's birthday--with hot dogs and Cheetos. Close by on the mainland, dark rain clouds hung on the peaks of the Andes Mountains creating a spectacularly dramatic sunset. A bright rainbow appeared over the mountains cascading even more color to the brilliant sky—one more gift for the birthday boy.

We departed before sundown the following day for an overnight passage to the islands of Las Aves located ninety-eight nautical miles to the north. As soon as I unfurled the jib sail we noticed a rip on the edge. That wasn't good. Ken and I agreed that it would be prudent to turn around, sail back through the reef to Isla Larga and re-anchor before dark. In the morning, at anchor, we unfurled the jib and lowered it to the deck. Luckily, the four-inch tear was in the protective reinforcing strip and not the actual sail. My temporary repairs would have to suffice until a sail maker back on Bonaire could stitch it properly.

Iniki was underway, again, at 3:00PM that afternoon. The wind was on our beam at ten to fifteen knots and increased to seventeen knots during the night with four-foot seas. It was a great sail. We hooked a nice cero mackerel at 10:00AM the next morning, just as we arrived at our destination. Jake now had saltwater running through his twelve-year-old veins and had no problem with seasickness. He was tan, sported a bandana on his head, pirate style, and a huge grin on his face as he reeled in the fish and posed for photographs.

This trip was our first visit back to Las Aves since battling the Christmas winds there the previous December. Now, in August, the area was a peaceful delight. The calm, crystal clear water revealed magnificent coral gardens abundant with sea life.

Following an overnight passage, there are three things that I want: a swim, some food and sleep—in that order. Once those needs were satisfied, the three of us were revived and ready to go snorkeling. Ken is a dead-on shot with a Hawaiian sling. The rubber is stretched and the spear released with a sling-shot effect. In no time at all Ken speared a fat black grouper to go with our mackerel for dinner. His grandson was thoroughly impressed, and so was I. Back on the boat there was a lot of Tim Allen/cave-man grunting going on as the men relived the hunt: "Man good hunter. Man get fish and bring to woman. Woman happy."

The feeling of self-sufficiency was exciting. The wind had carried us to that little bit of paradise, where we were anchored for free. We were changing the sea water into drinking water by reverse osmosis and had all the fresh seafood we could eat. The simplicity and satisfaction was profound. My living space on the boat was cozy with two people and tight with our grandson aboard. But when I stepped out into the cockpit on deck and surveyed the grand view in all directions, I had all the space I needed.

After that first spear fishing expedition, Jake couldn't wait to get back in the water the next day and learn to use the Hawaiian sling. "Let's go hunting, Papa!" He was very comfortable in the water and had no trouble diving six feet underwater with a snorkel to look for lobsters under the coral heads. Ken and Jake swam in one direction and I snorkeled off in another in search of lobsters.

Spiny lobsters are difficult to spot until you know what to look for. Hidden under the coral during the day, only the antennas are visible. If you tickle the antennas they may walk out of their hole to investigate. That's when you spear them. I couldn't find any that day. A few hundred yards away I heard a commotion from Ken and Jake. I figured they found one but I couldn't believe my eyes when they returned with their prize. The game bag was filled with the biggest lobster I had ever seen. That granddaddy must have weighed 20 lbs. (well, at least 15 lbs., anyway). Ken had to break off the antennas to get it in the bag. It was huge and so impressive that I felt a tinge of guilt and regret for ending its life. However, those feelings were quickly replaced with thoughts of the mouth-watering meal soon to be on our table. I steamed the legs for the first course, like crab legs. The tail was divided between the three of us. My portion was the size of a normal restaurant serving.

Jake said he wanted to stay in Las Aves for a long time. He became very proficient with the spear gun and learned how to fillet the fish. However, his summer vacation came to an end and we had to sail back to Bonaire and put him on an airplane back to California to begin the seventh grade. He went home with a good supply of stories and photos to back them up.

Chapter 10
Aruba to Colombia

October 24, 1998

Ken landed back in Bonaire after a weeklong business trip to Caracas, Venezuela. He walked out of the airport to the front curb and hailed a taxi to the waterfront downtown. Placing his bag in the backseat he sat up front and asked the driver how the weather had been the last week while he was gone. That's when he heard the news of the wind reversal caused by Hurricane Mitch.

About the same time I stepped off *Iniki* into the inflatable. I drove a short way to shore and tied up to the dinghy dock at Karel's Tiki Bar to wait for Ken. I missed him terribly. It had been four days since my all night ordeal with the storm and wind reversal. I was still skittish and worried that it would happen again. I planned to wait until we returned to the sailboat before I told my scary story. But since the cab driver mentioned the storm, Ken asked me about it immediately.

We loaded his luggage into the dinghy and I began to describe the episode as we headed out to the mooring. Another dinghy stopped along side *Iniki* just as we arrived. I didn't recognize the couple.

"Hi!" the man greeted us. "We just wanted to meet the woman who saved her boat single-handedly. Well done!"

"If that happened to me" the woman added, "our boat would have sunk. I could never do that."

I had become the talk of the local cruising community. In the locker room of the health club a Dutch woman was talking to me about how she and her husband fared the night of the storm. Their boat was in the marina and waves made it very uncomfortable. She continued, "And did you hear about the American woman who was alone and saved her boat all by herself?"

"No, what happened?" I asked wondering if I knew the woman. As I listened to her I suddenly realized that she was talking about *me*! She didn't know that I was "the American woman" that she was going on and on about.

The sight of the damaged boats on the shoreline was a powerful visual reminder of what could have happened to me. Afterwards, our cruising friends spoke to me with awe and new respect. Their perceptions of me reinforced the changes in self-image taking place in my own mind.

November 10, 1998

My parents were passengers on the Crystal Symphony cruise ship and were scheduled to stop in Aruba for a day. Ken and I were still in Bonaire, two islands away, when I told them we would sail over to rendezvous in Aruba. I warned that we couldn't guarantee that the weather would cooperate but would do our best to meet them.

We cleared out of Bonaire and sailed 55 miles west to Curacao. After anchoring overnight we continued westward to Aruba the next morning, sailing downwind in 6-10 foot seas. We arrived and cleared customs and immigration in Oranjestad, the capital of Aruba on the day before the cruise ship's scheduled arrival.

Aruba is a bustling, action-packed island compared to Bonaire. The ornate, brightly colored Dutch architecture in the downtown had become space for designer shops, jewelry stores, casinos and all the fast food chains. Fancy hotels and condominiums lined the beautiful beaches north of town. One to three cruise ships came into port everyday.

Ken and I woke very early in order to get ashore and be waiting on the big commercial pier when the Crystal Symphony docked. I made a "Welcome to Aruba, Tom & Jill" sign and held it up like the tour guides do. My folks were among the first to walk off the ramp, anxious to see if we had arrived in time. They spotted us right away.

My Dad wasn't interested in touring the island but thought it would be fun to go for a day-sail on *Iniki*. We shuttled them by dinghy out to the anchorage and had a blustery sail for an hour up to the beaches on the north side of the island. Dad took the helm and sailed in gusts up to thirty knots with all the form of a true Navy man.

Mom wasn't so confident. "Tom, don't you think you should let Ken take over?"

"He's doing great!" Captain Ken reassured her. My father grinned.

We anchored off one of the hotel beaches and I mixed up a rum punch while the others took a swim. There was time for lunch in a tiki bar built on stilts out over the water before we escorted them by cab back to the cruise ship in time to depart. At 5:00PM the huge ship followed the setting sun destined for the Panama Canal. It was a wonderful afternoon and it helped my parents better understand what our cruising life was like.

We remained in Aruba for a couple months and contemplated our next move. According to many experts, once a sailboat makes landfall in Aruba, there is no easy way to turn back to the eastern Caribbean. Many who have tried it say they would rather sail westward around the entire world than to venture eastward from Aruba into the boisterous trade winds and oncoming seas. Of course every year a few brave souls try it only to discover that their vessels and crew suffer a relentless pounding.

Our new plan was to sail southwest from Aruba to Colombia, then continue west to the San Blas Islands off the coast of Panama. Even though it was a downwind sail, getting there would be no picnic. The first leg to Cartegena was a non-stop voyage over 450 nautical miles through one of the most challenging regions of the Caribbean, with few safe ports of refuge. The Colombian coast is notorious for high winds and rough seas for a number of reasons. First, there is the land effect from the Andes Mountains and secondly, there are currents and counter-currents to contend with. The trade winds blow uninterrupted for over seven hundred miles before reaching that corner of the sea. Forty percent of the time, according to the Pilot Charts, the winds are at least thirty-five knots with twelve to fifteen foot seas. The guidebooks recommend staying twenty-five miles or more off the isolated Guajira Peninsula to avoid Colombian drug runners and pirates. We took the advice to heart even though there had not been any reported problems for a few years.

I was nervous about the probability of rough seas on this passage. It would also be longer than any previous passages we had done. We took extra care when securing everything on deck. My tension rose. Finally, I told Ken how I dreaded this passage. He went over the charts with me and reassured me that we would wait as long as necessary for a good weather window.

February 23, 1999

The winds suddenly eased and the weather forecasters predicted ideal conditions for our trip. We immediately got our exit papers stamped, and positioned ourselves for an early morning get-away.

At first light we hoisted the sails and turned *Iniki* westward. The conditions were perfect: clear blue sky, fifteen to twenty knots of wind out of the northeast with only three to six foot swells. I was able to relax and enjoy the sail. That first afternoon we saw a pod of spinner dolphins jumping ten feet out of the water. Some did complete head over tail flips while others spun horizontally in the air like a perfectly thrown football. These were not conditioned responses to a whistle blowing trainer. The dolphins were simply doing what they do in the wild for their own entertainment. It was a privilege to witness the show.

The idyllic conditions held through the night and into the second day. By the third afternoon we approached Santa Marta on the northern coast of Colombia and everything got more challenging. The winds steadily increased to thirty-five knots and the seas built to ten feet. A strong gust of wind blew our fishing line into the wind generator and the spinning blades quickly wrapped the line around about a million times before either of us could react. Goodbye lure! We sailed, with a double reefed main, a few miles off shore from the steep cliffs along the coastline. Ken consulted the charts and guidebooks looking for refuge from the wind and seas if the conditions deteriorated further. One of the guidebooks mentioned a short cut between the coast and Isla de la Aguja. It was a fairly narrow pass but safe as long as you "don't turn around once you are committed and watch out for the large rock in the middle of the passage".

I looked ahead through the pass and the whole picture made me extremely uneasy. Ken steered us inside the island. There was no turning back now. Once *Iniki* got between the island and the towering cliffs on the mainland we were in a virtual wind tunnel with gusts blasting through it at forty-five knots! Since we were sailing downwind we had secured the boom with a preventer to avert an accidental jibe. Suddenly the wind shifted. The preventer did its job but caused mainsail to back-wind. We were stuck. No longer racing forward, the wind and currents pushed the boat sideways toward the rocky shore at the base of the cliffs.

"Jane, you've got to gently release the preventer so the boom can swing over", Ken told me.

I cautiously inched my way out on deck from the cockpit and was quickly drenched with spray. I held on with one hand as I reached for the line that would free the boom. A "gentle release" was not in the scenario because there was so much pressure on the sail from the strong wind. *Why didn't I have my sailing gloves on?* I yanked two or three times before the line came free. The boom slammed over to the port side. The uncontrollable line burned through layers of skin on the palm of my hand and on the tips of four fingers. *My fingerprints are gone for good!*

The mainsail filled and *Iniki* surged forward. The winds registered forty-eight knots. *Iniki* was flying! My stinging hand was on fire. I had to get back to the cockpit while Ken maneuvered the boat around the mid-channel boulder and a dugout canoe that appeared out of nowhere. The wide-eyed fisherman gaped at us and paddled for all he was worth to get out of our way. *Where the heck did he come from and why was he out trying to paddle a dugout in that wind?* We missed him by a few feet. Ken looked back to see the man crossing himself.

I went below to attend to my singed hand. I ran cold water over it and tried not to freak out at the gross sight of my shredded flesh.

"Are you OK?" Ken hollered down to me. "I'm sorry I can't help you but I need you to take the helm. We seem to be on a collision course with a freighter heading in to Santa Marta."

I took the wheel with my good hand and Ken called the ship on the VHF radio. The Norwegian captain was very hard to understand. Ken hurried back on deck to handle the lines for a rapid turn to starboard, out of harm's way. *Enough, already! I can't handle any more excitement today!*

Hours later in the middle of the night, ten miles offshore from the mouth of the Magdalena River, *Iniki* was pooped by an impressive wave over our stern. That had never happened before. Ken and our "waterproof" Garmin GPS were soaked. Our GPS navigation system died instantly. Ken retrieved our backup GPS and turned it on. We hadn't used it in such a long time that it would not initialize. It didn't know where we were. Fortunately, Ken had just taken a fix and marked our position on our paper chart before the wave hit. I was so glad that Ken had pre-planned our navigation in detail before we left Aruba. When he spotted a ship that night Ken called on the radio and asked for a position. We were exactly where we thought we were and right on course.

At dawn, after a 75-hour passage, we approached our destination. The early morning haze lifted and the ancient stone wall surrounding the old city of Cartegena came into view. The harsh winds subsided and all but vanished as we motored past Boca Grande, the first wide entrance to the inner harbor. It looks inviting but early defenders of the city built a hidden submerged wall with a heavy underwater chain across the entire width of the obvious entrance to thwart attacks by pirates.

The real entrance, Boca Chica, was another six miles down the coast. The well-marked channel led us by modern hotels, high rise condominiums and the Colombian Armada (Navy Base) and finally back to the old city. We pulled into a slip at Club Nautico de Manga. A dockhand dove into the nasty looking water to tie two long stern lines to an underwater mooring. It was definitely not an easy in and out situation.

The familiar faces of cruising friends we had not seen for five months appeared on the dock to greet us. They invited us to join them on their boat for cocktails at 5PM that afternoon. They were leaving the next day for the Panama Canal so it was a quick catch-up of ports and sailing tales.

March 1, 1999

Signs of modern times appeared along side the die-hard traditional ways in Cartagena. Fishermen in leaky dugout canoes threw nets to catch fish in the water near marinas full of multimillion-dollar sport fishing boats. A small donkey pulled a rickety wooden cart down the cobblestone street laden with fruits. Clip-clop. Clip-clop. The old vender ignored an impatient honking taxi driver who swerved around him.

In Ciudad Viejo, the old central city, narrow cobblestone streets were lined with balconies overflowing with brilliantly colored bougainvilleas. The street names changed every block, which made it very confusing. Sidewalks were barely wide enough for one person. Open wooden doors revealed beautiful flowered courtyards and fountains hidden from the street.

Peddlers jostled for space on the tight streets and yelled out their wares in monotonous phrases with the last syllable drawn out and held: "Aguacate, mango, pinaaaaaaaaaas" (avocadoes, mangos, pineapples) There were cigarettes sold individually, Cuban cigars, watches, sunglasses, coconut milk, emeralds, iguana eggs on a string and honey sold in chunks of bees wax with live bees included! The funniest sight of all was a man weaving through traffic on a bicycle with a whole gutted fish propped on top of this head like a hat.

We toured the old cathedrals and forts, walked by the home of Nobel Prize winning author, Gabriel Garcia Marquez and saw the torture chambers of the Spanish Inquisition House. We ate wonderful seafood with coconut rice in romantic old world settings for one-third the price of Aruba. We even discovered a small gym where I worked out for nearly two hours with a personal trainer for the equivalent of $1.50. Ken also found a great deal on a pair of solar panels, which he ingeniously installed on our dodger.

After one month in Cartagena we were ready to sail again and headed fifteen miles south to a group of islands called the Rosarios. It was great to be in clean clear water again. We spent a week diving, fishing, hunting for lobsters and watching our amp meter register 10-15 amps from the new solar panels and wind generator combined. That meant we could keep the beer in the refrigerator cold without running the engine so much to charge the batteries; and that was a good thing!

Chapter 11
The San Blas Islands of Panama

May 5, 1999

It's a gray, rainy day--the slow and steady kind of rain that will continue for hours. The weather rolled in late last night with much bluster and noise. Thunder quickly followed brilliant flashes of lightning. Heavy rain pounded the deck above our berth. I lay awake and listened. The storm was not a major concern, just one of those raucous and rowdy thunderstorms like those I remember experiencing in the Midwest. I knew our CQR anchor was plowed deep into the sand with plenty of scope, but I still found the storm unsettling. I looked over at Ken. He was snoring away. *If he's not concerned, then I guess I don't need to worry.* By morning the wind and chop diminished, leaving in its place a dreary sky and persistent drizzle that hampered visibility all day.

The rainy season in Panama began in May and normally lasted until December. The torrential downpours topped off our water tanks and turned our dinghy into a bathtub in a matter of minutes. But even with the predictable afternoon rains there was still plenty of sunshine in Panama—hot, steamy sunshine resulting in verdant rain forests and lush islands that flourish with wild abandon. It was quite a contrast from the dry desert islands of Venezuela and the Netherlands Antilles, where months would pass without a drop of rain.

On April 8, 1999 we sailed 150 miles from the Rosarios in Colombia west to Panama. It was a fast, 21-hour downwind passage. After our all night sail the morning light revealed flying fish everywhere on our wet deck. We counted seventy-five fish, ranging in size from two to ten inches.

"Hey, I'll bet these would make good bait!" Ken declared, so we collected them in zip-lock bags and put them in the freezer.

The San Blas Islands cover over one hundred miles along the northern coast of Panama. The islands belong to the Kuna Indians, who control and protect their own territory and culture. Throughout history, the Kuna Indians have never been conquered by anyone. They continue to maintain a peaceful and harmonious balance between the modern world and their own ancient traditions--an amazing feat in the face of economic, social and cultural pressures from the outside.

Our first landfall was Isla Pinos. We sailed through the break in the reef and glided along the tranquil water that kissed a long, white-sand beach edged by thousands of coconut palms. My first look at the island left my mouth hanging open. It was as if we had just landed in the Garden of Eden. On the mainland, a couple miles away, an uninterrupted tangle of green foliage blended into the blue mountains of the Continental Divide, which runs through the Isthmus of Panama.

Sailing Cayuca

San Blas Islands

Iniki anchored in the San Blas Islands

We motored slowly around to the protected side of the island and found a good place to anchor. Gazing ashore, I saw thatch-roofed, bamboo huts in the village. It was only 7:30 AM but there was already much activity. Men paddled their cayucas (dugout canoes) from the island to the mainland, where they traveled to hunt or tend their farm plot. *Is this real or a Hollywood setting?* Tired and hungry after our overnight trip I cooked a hearty, breakfast of eggs and fried potatoes. I looked forward to peaceful sleep on a still boat. But when I closed my eyes, my mind and body continued to move with the motion of the twelve-foot seas that *Iniki* rode up and down all night. Even so, it didn't take long before we both fell into a coma-like sleep for a few hours.

When Ken and I woke, our personal batteries were recharged and we were anxious to see this new world around us. We launched the dinghy that had been on the foredeck for the passage and headed for a nearby beach on Isla Pinos. Three tiny Kuna women saw our approach and came to greet us with a smile and a handshake. They spoke to us in Spanish while several shy, yet curious children scurried around us.

"What is your name? Where did you come from?" they wanted to know.

All three women were dressed in the traditional Kuna fashion: a bright printed blouse with an intricate, hand-stitched design on the front and back, a printed sarong skirt, a red-and-yellow head scarf over their short, black hair, beaded bracelets from their wrists to elbows and from the ankles to their knees. On their faces, a black line was drawn down the center of their nose, and heavy red rouge colored their cheeks. Gold nose rings, gold earrings and a gold breastplate-style necklace completed the adornment. The wild combination was way over the top but, on these small women, it worked! They were beautiful.

The designs on the blouses worn by the Kuna women are called molas. Molas are described as reverse appliqués. Layers of colored cloth are basted together with black or maroon on top as the background. Designs are cut through the different layers, then the edges are turned under and hand stitched to reveal the bright under colors. More details are sewn on with minute chain stitch on the more elaborate works. The average size molas, which are worn on the front and back of the blouses, is about 13 X 16 inches and take a month or more to complete. The very best molas can take a year to make. Mola designs reflect the surrounding environment with birds, fish, plants and animals. The more I studied the molas, the more impressed I was with the complex handiwork. We were anxious to buy some.

Ken with Kuna women on Isla Pinos

San Blas Islands

Kuna Molas

Proper Kuna etiquette required a visit to the saila (chief) of the village upon arrival to an island. The saila is a powerful man and his word is law. Ken and I wanted to introduce ourselves, pay our respects and ask permission to anchor and look around. Ken asked the women on the beach where we could find the saila and one of the women motioned for us to follow her. Carrying a toddler on her hip, the woman led us down the white-powder beach, and then turned onto a well-worn path through the forest. Sunshine sparkled through the leaves and danced on the ground. The gentle breeze rattled the tops of the coconut palms. Shells and red flowering hibiscus plants lined the pathway. It was magical!

Soon we came to Tupak Village where about 200 Kunas lived. The dwellings seemed close together by our standards, but the rows of bamboo huts with thatched roofs were neat and tidy. A recreation area in the center of the village had a volleyball net set up. Volleyball is a game for tall athletes but no one informed the Kuna people. After the Pygmies, the Kunas are said to be the second smallest race of people on earth, yet they love to play volleyball.

The saila was in the "congresso", the large meeting hut where the entire village gathers every night to sort out any problems or disagreements. The saila presides over the meetings while swinging in a hammock in the center of the room. The villagers sit on benches positioned in circles facing the center. The headman spoke only Kuna and used an interpreter to speak Spanish to us. I suspect he spoke Spanish and possibly a little English as well, but chose to speak only the traditional language in his role as chief.

The man who translated for the chief was the official secretary for the village. He charged us a fee of $6.00 to anchor and gave us a stamped, signed receipt. The saila gave us permission to fish and catch lobster, and look around the village and the beaches. However, we were not allowed to walk around the rest of the island. He was still upset over some French cruisers who had recently taken mangos and coconuts without permission. It was forbidden to take any fruit, particularly coconuts—even if they were on the ground. Coconut trees were personal property and the coconuts were as good as cash, worth 25 cents each. One of the guidebooks equated taking coconuts to horse stealing in the Old West. The Kunas collected coconuts and bartered with them for flour, sugar, rice, milk powder and other staples from the Colombian trading boats. The Colombians took the coconuts to make coconut oil.

The secretary also informed us that if we wanted to buy any molas, the women would bring them to the congresso the next day. That arrangement would insure all women would have an equal chance to sell their work. We agreed and returned the next day.

The Kunas call foreigners "Merkies", which comes from the word "Americans". When Ken and I walked through the village we often heard, "Hola, Merkie!" coming from inside the bamboo huts or from brave, smiling children who ran up, touched us, then scampered away. "Hola, Merkie!" Once we arrived at the meetinghouse, the secretary took a bullhorn up and down the village lanes, shouting in Kuna. He probably said something like, "Merkies buying molas! Bring everything you've got right now!" Immediately, women, young and old, hurried over with arms full of molas. Some hung their work on poles inside the dimly lit hut. Others just held them up for our examination. What a sight! Each mola was truly a work of art. Ken and I were overwhelmed trying to decide which to buy. Of course, every woman wanted us to buy *her* molas. Cruisers don't often visit the remote villages like this one, so the Kuna women viewed us as a financial godsend. The only cash these families ever saw was from the sale of their molas. Everything else came from trading coconuts.

Horatio proudly shows his diploma

Horatio's daughter

Fish we caught and shared with the Saila on Isla Pinos

Tupak Village, Isla Pinos

Cayucas on the beach, Isla Pinos

Our Mola purchases

On our first visit to the village we met a man who was anxious to practice speaking English with us. Horatio was sixty-six years old and had lived his whole life on that island. He learned English from a correspondence course he took as a teenager. Horatio proudly showed us his framed diploma and old lesson books from the Hemphill School in Los Angeles dated 1946! Welcoming the opportunity to speak English, he invited Ken and me to his house to meet his family. Over the next several days we met with Horatio and got a better feeling for their way of life. Whenever Horatio heard a word he was unfamiliar with, he took out a little notebook and wrote down the word and definition. During one visit Ken noticed an old foot pedal Singer sewing machine, which hadn't worked in years. Ken fixed the bobbin, rethreaded the machine and got it working once again. The women were thrilled to be able to use it to piece their blouses together. From that moment on, the villagers thought Ken was a mechanical genius for fixing the antique. Word spread and people began to bring him all sorts of things to fix--mostly radios and audiotape players with batteries either dead or missing. They thought Ken's electrical test meter was magical and they spoke in hushed tones whenever he used it.

Ken repairs an old sewing machine

Traditional Kuna Dance on Isla Pinos

Ken donates his reading glasses

Horatio's wife was in constant motion. She tended the cooking fire in their cooking/eating hut (separate from the sleeping hut) using dried coconut husks for fuel. She grated coconut meat, carried water, washed utensils and swept dirt from the houses. Big mounds of coconuts, avocados and plantains lay close by. When the women weren't taking care of the children or cooking, they made molas. The molas-in-progress were carried everywhere and worked on whenever the women sat down.

Horatio's 85-year-old father swung in a hammock in the eating hut, where he witnessed all the action. A daughter and daughter-in-law also lived in the family compound with their children. Their husbands were away somewhere working to earn money for their families.

On another day Ken and I saw two fishermen arrive at the pier with their cayucas full of fish. A call went out to the village and soon all the women appeared carrying baskets or plastic containers. The women lined up their containers on the dock, then sat down to patiently wait. The two fishermen proceeded to count and equally divide the catch by number, size and variety. Each household got its fair share of fresh fish.

Everyone we met on Isla Pinos was very tolerant of our presence and questions, as long as we respected their ways and rules. Many went out of their way to be friendly and communicate with us. The Kuna people are warm, intelligent, curious, and we enjoyed their wonderful sense of humor.

Kuna Children

Another perfect anchorage in the San Blas Islands

There were many more islands to visit and explore, so we said goodbye and prepared to move on. We meandered west along the coast and visited other villages and beautiful uninhabited islands with strange sounding names: Ustupu, Achutupu, Mamitupu, Nusatupu, and Kuanidup. The scenery was stunning. Every direction I looked could easily have been a spectacular photo pick for the cover of "Island" magazine.

When we anchored near the island of Rio Sidra, an old man missing several teeth paddled up alongside our boat and gave us some mangos as a gift. He spoke English and he turned out to be the saila of Rio Sidra. He had been tending his coconut plantation on the mainland. He invited us to visit him when we went ashore, which we did, and he proudly answered our many questions about Kuna customs and traditions.

As a clinical hypnotherapist who is an expert on the subject of altered states of consciousness and the power of suggestion, Ken was very interested to meet a local nele, as the Kuna witchdoctors are called. He asked Carlos, the chief, if he would introduce us to the nele in his village. Neles were said to possess special powers and were very important people in the Kuna villages. They had an intimate understanding of medicinal plants and collected jungle plants, tree bark, roots and even minerals and bones to use to heal the sick. They also used carved wooden statues called "nuchus" in their healing process. After the wooden nuchus are carved, a kantule or chanter sings to them for seven days and nights in order to "open" the statue's eyes. Once the nuchu's eyes were opened, the Kunas believed that the nuchu was a living spirit that traveled around at night, all seeing and all knowing.

When a patient was brought to the nele's hut for a cure, he or she rocked in a hammock while the nele smoked a mixture of tobacco and coca leaves and communicated with the nuchus. The nele believed that a person got sick because part of their soul was missing. The nuchus searched at night to locate and retrieve the missing part of their soul. Nuchus also communicated with the nele to reveal when something was going to happen in the near future that would have an impact on the village. The nele in turn let the saila know. The chief and the witch doctor made a powerful team!

Ken & Carlos, the chief of Rio Sidra

New friend, Basante with wife and baby.

Young girls come to our boat to sell their molas

After our conversation and monetary contribution to the village, Carlos invited us to watch the celebration of a girl's puberty rite. *Oh, no! Do I want to witness this? There are some horrendous things done to children around the world in rites of passage. What were we in for?* Ken's questions prompted the chief to educate us. When a girl reached the age of thirteen to fifteen years old, she had a ceremony where a female priest cut the girl's hair. The girl was then considered to be a woman, started to wear the traditional outfit and was available for marriage. *What a relief! No horrible mutilation involved, so this ought to be very interesting.*

The puberty rite party was held in a "chicha" house and lasted four days and four nights. Chicha is a strong drink made from fermented sugarcane. Since we were outsiders Ken and I were not allowed inside the hut, but we watched through the doorway. The men were together on one side of the hut, wearing dress shirts with neckties and hats. The women were on the other side of the room in their traditional clothes. The men and women smoked tobacco from little pipes and drank chicha from gourds. Every now and then a small group stood up, filled their gourds with chicha and passed them to others who then started chanting and dancing in a circle to call the gods.

In the center of the hut between the men and women, four men sat smoking cocoa leaves. Suddenly, they jumped up and danced around, shaking their heads and bodies to rattle the bundle of bones that dangled around their necks. One of the four proceeded to blow smoke on some nuchus that had been placed under some banana leaves. The rituals were repeated over and over. Ken and I watched for an hour when suddenly the men all left the chicha hut in a single file. The man in front carried a lantern and led the group off somewhere. Next, the women filed out and went the opposite direction. Curious, Ken asked the chief where they were going.

"To take a piss," the saila said matter-of-factly.

When the groups returned to the chicha hut the drinking, smoking and dancing continued. We wondered about fights and arguments with all the non-stop drinking. Carlos said that if someone got nasty, he or she was told to go home and sleep. If that person ignored the warning they were fined one chicken, which they had to kill, clean and present to the saila.

The "happy day" continued all night and for days to follow. Ken and I left them to their celebration and returned to our boat amazed by what we had witnessed.

We often had Kuna visitors come to our boat to visit. They were as inquisitive about us and we were about them. They were delighted to look at photographs of our family. The Kunas who were too shy to come right up to our boat hovered nearby in their cayucas, apparently content to just watch us. After a few days all the attention prompted us to move on and find a little privacy at some of the uninhabited islands.

Exploring a river in Kuna Yala on mainland Panama

Unique bird nest along the river

Kuna burial ground on the mainland

Valuable coconut palms

We were in the San Blas Islands for an entire month before we even saw another cruising boat! After six weeks we found the favorite anchorage of cruisers in the area. The East Holandes Cays were about seventy miles from Isla Pinos, where we made our first stop. Arriving in East Holandes we found six other sailboats anchored in a protected pool surrounded by four small, uninhabited islands. On each one, coconut palms leaned out over a smooth sandy beach, as if trying to find breathing room away from the dense cluster of trees in the island's center. Beyond the island, the surf crashed onto a thriving coral reef. Ken couldn't wait to get in the water to explore the new hunting area. The reef was teaming with fat grouper, big snapper, large red coral crabs and monstrous lobsters. Of course, there were very large barracuda and sharks as well, but they left us alone. The place had it all: good holding, clear water, wind protection, food, sandy beaches, and idyllic scenery. To top it off, there were other women to talk to--in English--aboard the other sailboats! My dear husband is a marvelous sailing companion but I was ready for some socializing.

We lingered in paradise for a couple of weeks, enjoying our new friends. There were beach barbeques, book swaps and trash-burning parties. A few boat chores were accomplished but mostly we relaxed. I wanted to soak up the pristine beauty all around me through every one of my pores and hold onto it forever.

Coral crab for two!

Chapter 12
The Diagnosis

June 26, 1999

Dark, ominous thunderheads gathered over the distant mountains on the mainland of Panama at the periphery of our sunny island paradise. I noticed their development as Ken and I prepared to anchor our sailboat 25 yards off the inviting beach on Kuanidup in the San Blas Islands. We had to be ever watchful of clouds that hovered at the edge of our existence. Sometimes they progressed out over the islands on the Caribbean side of the isthmus with violent storms.

All boaters know that weather conditions can change rapidly. One minute all is calm and peaceful, then--WHAM! --we are slammed down and shaken up with a reality check. At sea, it can come in the form of a sudden wind shift and foul weather. The winds of my balmy life were about to shift again. The previous year in Bonaire, an unforeseen storm descended on me when I was alone. I was forced into action when all I really wanted to do was close my eyes and pretend everything was OK. The situation was terrifying for me but I managed to get through it safely by focusing on one step at a time.

From our anchorage in the San Blas I watched the black clouds creep closer. If my life were a screenplay, the descending darkness would have been an effective foreshadowing technique. I didn't see the omen. I just closed the hatches and portholes in preparation for the approaching rain that I could smell in the air. My thoughts were on our up-coming visit to the United States. Our daughter, Tina was to be married in August. In a couple weeks we would fly home to help out with final wedding plans before the exciting event.

We spent nearly eight weeks cruising around the San Blas Islands and were reluctant to leave Kuna Yala. But there was no place to leave our sailboat in that area so we were forced to move on. Sailing along the coast we stopped in Jose Pobre (Poor Joe) Bay, which was twenty nautical miles from the entrance to the Panama Canal. There we met Marco, a Swiss adventurer who sailed all over the world until he found his own personal paradise in Panama. In tiny Jose Pobre,

Marco swallowed the anchor and moved ashore. He bought an acre of jungle shoreline and built the quaint and very rustic Marco's Marina and Restaurant. I use the term "Marina" very loosely because it was simply a few moorings behind a reef. Marco served ice-cold beer and prepared some great meals in his little open-air kitchen.

July 12, 1999

Colon was the closest city. It was a three hour drive. Every week Marco made the trip to town for food and supplies. With *Iniki* closed up and secure behind some mangroves, Ken and I hitched a ride to Colon with Marco. From there we could hire a taxi to drive us to the airport in Panama City in order to fly back the States. The first hour of the drive from Jose Pobre to Colon was painfully slow. Our able driver cajoled the old car through deep ruts and around boulders on the steep, rough, road through the jungle. Once we reached the paved road the remainder of the drive was easy.

After living on "island time" in third world countries it was a culture shock to return to the United States. For the previous two months that we sailed waters of Panama, Ken and I were immersed in an untamed and undeveloped world. Many places we visited were accessible only by boat. Wild and free creatures surrounded us--howler monkeys in the treetops, shrieking sea birds, playful dolphins. I craved the wide-open spaces and grand vistas, needing them like air and water. The sudden arrival in the land of plenty and fast paced efficiency was met with mixed feelings. I was excited to be home but then after a few days in civilization I found myself missing the serenity of our life on the water.

From the moment we landed in the States that July I noticed little things that were a huge contrast from rural Panama and Colombia—the smooth paved roads and clear directional signs; so many choices on the supermarket shelves. Who knew grocery shopping could be so exciting? Many details I had previously taken for granted were now viewed through knowing appreciative eyes. It felt good, on one hand, to return home to the familiar ways and language. However, I soon realized that our journey had changed our perspective on living and shifted our priorities. It was an odd sensation to watch family and friends race around accomplishing much in a single day. I used to be the same way before I left on this adventure. Now I had the urge to grab hold of the workaholics, force them to sit still for a moment and relax. I felt claustrophobic inside houses with the windows closed and draperies drawn after my life in constant fresh air, wide-open spaces, sunshine, rain or whatever the day delivered.

July 15, 1999

Our first stop in the States was a visit with family in the Chicago area. I happily made dates to see friends and looked forward to the approaching wedding in California.

Mixed in with the fun were appointments for teeth cleaning, contact lens check and a mammogram. At the imaging center where I had gotten mammograms for several years, there was a radiologist on staff who read the results immediately. Nurses delivered a carnation with a clear report to women waiting in the changing room. I sat in the waiting room flipping through a magazine. The door opened. "Mrs. Grossman?"

I looked up. There was no flower in the nurse's hand. "The doctor would like to do an ultrasound for a better look." she explained as she led me to another room.

Dr. Kim showed me the films and pointed out the star shape that concerned her.

"I see this very suspicious looking mass in your left breast. It wasn't present on your last mammogram. I don't like the looks of it. I think it is important that you see a surgeon and get a tissue sample as soon as possible."

My heart pounded. The dreaded word that was left unsaid-- "CANCER"-- screamed inside my head. I left the office in a daze. I think I called my husband but I don't remember. The surgeon who removed benign lumps in the past had an office two floors down in the same building. My mind reeled as I opened the door to the surgical group to make an appointment.

"When would you like to come in, Mrs. Grossman?" the receptionist asked with the proper balance of cheerfulness and concern.

I could hardly speak. I couldn't think. *CANCER. BREAST CANCER!* Ken and I had planned to drive to Indiana in two days to visit my sister. I scheduled the appointment after that short trip but by the time I drove back to my in-law's house I knew I couldn't wait a week. The waiting and wondering would drive me crazy. And maybe time was of the essence. I called the surgeon's office back and took the soonest appointment on Monday morning. It would be a very long weekend.

Fran, my mother-in-law was beside herself when she heard the news. Ken did not want anyone to jump to conclusions, as we did not have all the facts. I put on a mask of nonchalance around the house and wondered if I fooled anyone. That night as I lay in bed with Ken the tears that were just below the surface all afternoon spilled over when I admitted my fear to my husband.

"I'm so scared."

Ken held me close and said, "We got through the last scare and we'll get through this one. What's the worst that could happen?"

I thought for a second and responded, "I could have cancer and die!" Then, surprisingly, I started laughing. I said it out loud. The big "it" was out in the open and I realized how pointless it was to catastrophize the situation without all the facts.

I attempted to distract myself all weekend to avoid thinking about the huge unknown hanging over me. We visited friends and rented videos. By Monday morning I could feel myself turning inward. I could no longer maintain the inane pretext that everything was fine. The optimist in me struggled. *How could I possibly have something so ominous and deadly*

*growing inside me when I feel so fit and healthy? It's not happening to me.
Surely, the lump is harmless. I can't even feel it. But what if...No! Don't
even go there.*

Ken drove me to my appointment. The surgeon confirmed the need for
a tissue sample and scheduled an ultrasound guided needle biopsy for the
next day. A radiologist with local anesthetic performed the procedure.

I had to wait two more days for the results—an eternity. I spent the
remainder of the day on the couch with an ice pack watching comedy
videos. *Maybe I can get through this if I can just keep laughing.* I was
showered with phone calls that afternoon from family and friends around
the country and even from Caracas, Venezuela (news travels fast through
the Grossman grapevine). It was a comfort to receive such an outpouring
of love and concern.

The next day I was sore but determined to go as planned to visit my sister,
Nancy and her family in Indiana. I gave her phone number to my doctor so he
could call me there with the biopsy results. Ken suggested I heal another day
before we made the three-hour drive in our bumpy Jeep Wrangler with no air
conditioning.

"No," I insisted. "I want to go today."

I hadn't seen my sister for a year and I needed to talk to her in person.
Nancy was a registered nurse with a degree in psychology. I often turned to
her for grounding and advice when I became confused or unsure of myself. I
could always count on her frank, common sense and humor to help me regain
my footing.

The temperature reached a sizzling 101 degrees that day in Ft. Wayne,
Indiana. Ken and I shared stories and pictures of Panama and listened to all the
activities of our four teenage nieces and nephews. We laughed and ate comfort
food.

July 22, 1999

The day dragged while I watched the clock and waited for the phone. My
surgeon called at 6:30pm. I went into a bedroom to take the call in private. He
got right to the point.

"The tissue samples show cancer cells."

Cancer. CANCER. The word echoed in my ear. I had convinced myself
that nothing was wrong. *Did I hear him correctly? What was he saying now?* I
struggled to focus.

"...another appointment. In the mean time you can think about your options:
1. Mastectomy or 2. Lumpectomy with node removal and radiation."

Ken walked into the room looking for a sign. I looked at him and gave him a
thumb down signal. The doctor was still talking but my brain was a jumble and
I could not follow.

"....Do you have any questions? " I heard the gentle voice ask.

"I don't know. Can you repeat what you just said to my husband?"

I gave the phone to Ken. Visions of a dying friend came back vividly. My mind's eye saw her emaciated near death attached to an oxygen tank after a courageous ten-year battle with breast cancer. I squeezed my eyes shut to rid myself of that image. I was not prepared to hear that diagnosis. Who could be? It knocked the wind out of my sails and left me in irons, gasping for air.

Ken hung up the phone and hugged me, also stunned by the news. My brother-in law hugged me. Nancy immediately laid out a plan of action to get me focused and keep me from falling into the big dark void of hopelessness.

"Your attitude right now is extremely important." she instructed. "You need to take control, find out all the facts and all your options so YOU are able to make decisions about what is best for you. You are not a victim at the mercy of the almighty doctors! You interview and hire the best doctors to be on your team to cure you. YOU are the boss."

I sat staring and nodded in agreement but I thought, *Oh Shit! I don't want this. Dear God, I'm scared!*

"Is it OK if I cry before I get tough?" I squeaked as my emotional defenses crumbled.

When the tears ceased I pulled myself together to make some difficult phone calls to my parents, Ken's parents, our daughters and my other sister. I hated to worry them with the frightening news but I knew I was going to need all their love and support in the months to come.

I did not sleep well that night. I got up early and quietly left the house for a walk. I wanted to be alone for a while. I was still in shock and not sure how I was supposed to feel. The act of placing one foot in front of the other and breathing the morning air offered some comfort. The birds continued to sing their sweet songs. Frogs still croaked in the pond. Life went on. So must I.

After breakfast my family research team and I huddled around the computer and pulled up tons of information on breast cancer, disease stages, treatment options, clinical trials, drugs, support groups and chat lines. When I couldn't read anymore—I could only handle the mental load in small doses--I printed out several more pages to read later. It was very confusing to read all the medical information about the insidious disease. I still didn't want to believe I belonged in that group of seriously ill people. I felt physically strong and healthy. I never smoked. I exercised, ate healthy foods and was rarely sick. I could not reconcile the latest conflicting data with my self-image.

I indulged myself with one more day of encouragement and support, humor and laughter. I was then ready to return to Chicago to get on with it. There were long hugs and more tears at the door before Ken and I left. Nancy held my shoulders, looked me in the eye and said, "You can do this, Jane, because you are the strongest, bravest person I know."

That statement astounded me. I was forty-five years old but I always felt like the little sister who could never quite measure up to my older sister. And here she was, telling me that I was strong and brave. I didn't see myself that way, but if Nancy said it was so, maybe I could get through this ordeal. I grabbed hold of her words and hung on for dear life!

Chapter 13
Surgery

August 5, 1999

I learned that my cancer was "infiltrating ductal carcinoma". According to my Internet research 85% of breast cancers are ductal carcinoma. I made an appointment with another surgeon for a second opinion. Both concurred that I was a good candidate for the less invasive lumpectomy. I also made appointments with two oncologists who both were highly recommended. My decision on who to trust with my life, ultimately boiled down to my gut feeling and my comfort level concerning their accessibility and willingness to "be there" for me.

I called Dr. Philip Hoffman at the University of Chicago Hospital Center for Advanced Medicine and asked him to lead my team of experts to cure me. Dr. Hoffman's treatment plan consisted of surgery followed by four courses of chemotherapy and then 30 radiation treatments. *Twelve weeks of Chemo and six weeks of radiation.* The length of time involved sunk in. Ken and I left *Iniki* in Panama for a three-week visit home. Now we would be in Chicago for seven months. If all went well, it would be February before we saw our sailboat again. And that meant we were in for cold and snow on top of everything else.

The word "chemotherapy" is one of those trigger words for terror. I don't recall ever hearing anything pleasant about chemotherapy. Baldness and puking were my associated images. I forced those thoughts from my mind. *I can't think about that now. It's too much. I'll just concentrate on one step at a time.*

The first step was surgery. I wanted the cancer out of my body as soon as possible. But there was our daughter's wedding in California to consider as well as a full surgical schedule at the hospital. My doctors agreed that one-month delay would not do any harm, so my surgery would be after the wedding.

August 14, 1999

I found the wedding ceremony and festivities profoundly moving. Facing my own mortality placed an extra significance on this celebration of love and life. I cherished the "mother-daughter moments" I had with Tina as we made bows and decorations for the church and outdoor reception. Ken was so proud and handsome in his tux as he walked the lovely bride down the aisle. It was a joy to see her happiness and to welcome a new son-in-law into the family.

Throughout the festivities, unsettling questions lingered persistently in the back of my mind. *How far had my cancer progressed? Would I live to be 100 and dance at many more weddings or could this be my last?* These thoughts changed the way I looked at everything and left me in a twilight zone. Even in the midst of the crowds of jubilant wedding guests I felt like a detached observer.

August 19, 1999

After the wedding Ken and I flew back to Chicago and talked about where we would stay for the next six months. We considered renting an apartment, then Ken's parents generously offered to have us stay with them. I worried that my troubles would be a burden for them. On the other hand we could be a big help as they were both in their eighties.

Fran and Walter Grossman convinced us that they really wanted us to stay with them. We fixed up the second story of their little bungalow where Ken and 11 siblings grew up. We replaced the carpeting and painted the dark knotty pine paneling a cheery yellow called "Caribbean Sun" (the name sold me). The area was transformed into a cute and cozy bedroom and sitting room.

Luckily for me, my husband has a Ph.D. in Clinical Hypnotherapy. Tapping into his talents proved to be a priceless resource for recovery and healing. Ken recorded the first of several self-hypnosis tapes for me. On the first tape his soothing voice relaxed me and filled me with feelings of being loved by my family and friends. I listened to suggestions to heal quickly after surgery and visualized microscopic armies traveling throughout my body on a mission to find the cancer, cut it out and kill it. *I am cancer-free.* Everyday I hypnotized myself with Ken's tapes, which helped me to remain positive, calm and relaxed--a daunting task when my mind kept returning to the big unknown that lay before me. I didn't want to think negative thoughts or acknowledge my fears that the cancer had spread elsewhere in my body, but it was impossible to stop the thoughts.

My good friend, Ann, who I've known since grade school, called to offer support and answer my questions. She had been down the breast cancer road a couple years earlier. Ever since fifth grade she could make me laugh and had a gift to see the humor in the most serious subjects so as not to be done in by them. I will never forget her insight and advice:

"People will want to do things for you. They will want to help but they won't know how. So I say 'USE your cancer'! Get all you can get out of it."

August 24, 1999

It was the day before my surgery and the phone rang continually. My parents, my sisters, my pals, my daughters, my in-laws, my minister all called to tell me they were praying for me. Ken's parents, sister and visiting nieces and nephews gave me a giant gift bag filled with things for my hospital stay and recovery: a soft comfortable fleece outfit, peppermint tea, chocolate, gummy bears, a book and a candle in a coconut shell to remind me of the islands. It was perfect. Tears streamed down my cheeks prompting a group hug from all present. I felt so blessed to have so much love and kindness around me in my time of need. I felt as though I was cradled in warm, protective, loving arms. For the first time I was not afraid. I felt at peace.

August 25, 1999

I listened to my hypnosis tape before Ken drove me to the hospital. The nurse who checked me in and prepared me must have been an undercover angel sent to help me through the difficult day ahead. Her name was Marianne and she chatted with me to get some background information as well as to put me at ease, I suspect. Ken was at my side and did his best to elevate me from patient number status to a memorable human being with an unusual life. He was convinced it would get me more attention and better treatment. When Marianne heard that we lived on a sailboat, had recently flown in from Panama and then I caught this lump with a routine mammogram, her response made me think. The most common response I heard to that information was "Oh, I'm sorry" or "How awful", "That's too bad".

Marianne replied, "Well, somebody is sitting on YOUR shoulder watching out for you!" *Hmmm. What a positive way to look at it.* By the time a technician from radiology came to fetch me this kind woman was holding my hand.

"I'm not supposed to do this," she said as she kissed me on the cheek. "I'm sure everything will turn out OK for you and you will be back sailing again soon."

I appreciated the warm uplifting attitude. It was as important as taking my vital signs, especially since I hadn't been checked into a hospital since I was three months old.

Ken gave me a kiss. "See you soon. I'll be right here."

An orderly wheeled my bed down an empty hallway to radiology where a thin wire was inserted into my breast to locate the tumor for the surgeon. The next stop was the Nuclear Medicine Department for the first step of a Sentinal Node Biopsy, a rather new procedure at that time.

I closed my eyes and imagined lying on a beach in the warm sun. The beautiful San Blas Islands were easy to recall. I focused my concentration on the rustling palm trees, the sound of the waves on the sand, the smell of the sea. Low-level radioactive dye was injected into my breast. A camera tracked the dye as it traveled to the lymph nodes under my left arm. The sentinal nodes, or first nodes to which the cancer cells might spread are then identified. Removal of those specific nodes allows for more detailed examination and avoids random extraction of unaffected lymph nodes.

The male technician and male radiologist informed me that there would be "some discomfort—like bee stings" when the dye was injected. *That doesn't sound too bad. In a few hours this whole thing will be over.* "Bee stings" proved to be the understatement of the hour. I lost my beach visions and was ready to confess to anything. A wand like a Geiger counter followed the blips of radioactive dye inside me. Three sentinal nodes were located and literally outlined on my skin with a black marker.

I saw Ken for a few minutes before proceeding to surgery. When I woke I was being lifted into a bed in the hospital room. My surgeon came in and announced everything went well.

"We got a clear margin on the tumor. There was no swelling in the lymph nodes and that's a very good sign."

More luck on my side! After one night in the hospital I was most anxious to get out of there. Before I left, I was surprised to have a visit from Marianne, the nurse who checked me in. She tracked me down to wish me well. I thought again about the profound effect her caring gestures, which went beyond the expected, had on me.

Ken drove me home at 10:30 the next morning. Pain pills knocked me out so I slept off and on the rest of the day. Ken was exhausted from worry and not sleeping well. I kicked him out of our bed so he wouldn't bump me or upset the drain tube under my arm. He spent two nights on the couch. He was devoted to my comfort and well being.

On the third day the drain tube was annoying me and I wanted it out.

"What can I get you, Jane? What would make you feel better?" my attentive husband inquired.

"I want my mom!" I whined, only half joking. "I want my mom to rub my back and make everything all better. And I want comfort food."

"You just name it", Ken said, "and I'll get it for you."

"I want roast chicken, mashed potatoes and gravy and a hot fudge sundae." I said dreamily as I trudged back to the bedroom to lie down, knowing that no one in that house would be cooking a big feast that day.

When I woke from my nap Ken had returned loaded down with bags full of goodies. He served up a plate of food from several carry out containers and I had my roasted chicken dinner, as requested, complete with dessert and the latest *People Magazine.*

August 31, 1999

Ken drove me to my follow up appointment with the surgeon who gave me the good news:

Tumor – 1.5 centimeters with a clear margin

Stage 1 – nothing in the lymph nodes

No micro-metastasis

I was momentarily speechless as the words confirmed the previous unofficial report. Relief and joy washed over me as my eyes met Ken's. I would have done cartwheels or jumped up and down on the spot had it not been for the damned drain tube still attached to me.

"Now, can you take this thing out of me before I rip it out myself?" I gleefully asked the doctor.

He instructed me on care and precautions to avoid lymphadema. It was very important to exercise my arm to regain full range of motion. Ken and I both thanked him profusely which he modestly shrugged off as "luck".

I called everyone to share my good news. I wanted to celebrate! The first step of my treatment was behind me. The cancer was gone from my body. The remaining treatments would be a powerful one-two punch to prevent any reoccurrence. I said, "Bring it on!" *I don't EVER want to go through all this again.*

That night I had a powerful dream that I remembered with vivid detail. I dreamt that I was in a house full of people. My whole family was there along with Ken, daughters, friends and strangers. People were coming and going from room to room. I noticed a mountain lion walk stealthily into the house without a roar or any display of aggression. I watched as it snuck into a side room, lay down and went to sleep. Everyone who had seen it worried about where the lion went ---was it dangerous? Is it still there? Finally, I asked my father if the lion was still in the side room. He went to look. My dad returned and told me he thought the lion was sleeping at first but he went closer and kicked it. It was dead.

My dad said to me, "You don't have to worry about it anymore."

Now I'm no psychiatrist, but the message to myself was quite clear—the cancer was dead and gone!

Chapter 14
Chemotherapy

September 13, 1999

I noticed the bald woman in the baseball cap as soon as Ken and I entered the cafeteria in the Center for Advanced Medicine at the University of Chicago Hospital. She wore makeup and earrings and looked almost natural. *That's what I'll do. I frequently wear baseball caps on the sailboat so it will feel normal to wear one after I lose my hair.*

A few minutes earlier Ken and I had left the oncology department, where I had an appointment with Dr. Philip Hoffman. He read the pathology report from my surgery, and discussed his recommended treatment: four courses of chemotherapy with Adriamycin and Cytoxan each three weeks apart, followed by radiation five days a week for six weeks, and then 20 mg of Tamoxifin every day for the next five years.

As I sat in the cafeteria, doctors, nurses and medical technicians came and went, stethoscopes hanging around their necks or poking out of the pockets of their lab coats. My thinking was slow and foggy. The doctor's words settled in and replayed in my mind—*blood test...heart function test...possible side effects... chemotherapy...anti-nausea pills... fatigue...hair loss...radiation...five years on pills...*Looking down that long road ahead of me, I felt the panic bubbling up from my gut. The whole picture was too much to cope with and way too scary.

Ken saw the tears in my eyes. "What's wrong?"

I couldn't speak of it. Not yet. *Don't think about it now. Keep breathing. Think only about the next small step and nothing else. I can do that much.*

The woman in the baseball hat clutched her husband's arm as he led her out the door. I blinked hard and wiped my eyes. *Don't lose it here. Get a grip.*

"I want to get out of this building," I said. "I need some fresh air *now.*"

Once in the car, away from the public eye, I let go and cried. I attempted to explain my thoughts and feelings to Ken.

"Do you want to go to a support group?" he asked.

"No. I don't think I can handle other people's troubles on top of my own. I don't want to focus on the disease. I don't want to give this cancer any power over me by dwelling on it. I don't want to admit to being a Cancer Patient."

About this time many articles appeared in newspapers and magazines about an incredible athlete who went through treatment for widespread cancer, survived and rebounded to win the grueling Tour de France bicycle race. Lance Armstrong became my hero and inspiration. I saved every article about him and cheered him on. I wondered how many others, like me, Lance had inspired.

September 14, 1999

News headlines reported that hurricane Floyd flogged the Bahamas and threatened the Florida coastline. Ken worried about *Iniki*. Our sailboat was safe from hurricanes in Panama, but we needed to get word to Marco about our delayed return. There was no phone in the village so Ken emailed a friend at Panama Yacht Services, who drove for three hours to personally deliver our message and phone number to Marco in Jose Pobre. Finally, a collect call came from Panama. *Iniki* was fine and Marco said he would be happy to watch over the boat, run the engines once a week and air it out.

In Illinois the morning air was now cold. The furnace in the house kicked on for the first time this season, creating that funny smell. There was a familiarity about cool autumn nights, sleeping under cozy comforters with crisp, fresh air seeping in under the windows opened just a crack. It was like an old friend I hadn't seen in a while. The smells brought to mind pumpkins and cornstalks, mums and apple cider, crunching leaves and football. I decorated the house and our upstairs area with flowers and gourds, in order to surround myself with pleasant things.

As my first chemotherapy session drew closer, I had trouble sleeping. It frightened me to read about the Adriamycin-Cytoxan cocktail that would be going into my body. The possible side effects were many. I asked Ken to make a new self-hypnosis tape for me to listen to. Instead of remaining passive and worrying about the poisons being injected into my body, I became the aggressor. During self-hypnosis with Ken's guided imagery I visualized the drugs as little army guys deployed to fight my battle—a seek-and-destroy mission to rid my body of any remaining cancer cells. I directed the action. I was in charge, not a victim. It was an important distinction in order to feel some semblance of control.

September 21, 1999

It was the day of my first chemo treatment. I woke early, went for a walk and listened to my tape.

"I guess I'm ready. Let's get this over with," I said to Ken.

We took the Stevenson Expressway into the city, then drove south on Lake Shore Drive to the University of Chicago campus. In the chemo ward of the medical center, a tall male nurse led me to a chair to have my blood pressure checked. I looked around and saw people lying in beds and pink recliner chairs, getting chemotherapy. One man had a shunt in his chest with an IV drip. The patients looked gray-skinned, bald and sickly.

My heart began to pound. My blood pressure rose. It was as though my breath was being sucked out of me. *I can't breathe.* I didn't want to be associated with all those sick people. I didn't want to sit in a pink recliner and be one of them. I panicked! I wanted to stand up and run. *I can't do this.* Terror gripped me.

Machines and equipment crowded each cubicle. Nurses unlocked drawers to retrieve syringes and vials of liquid, then re-locked the drawers with jingling keys. The male nurse told me to go to chair number 22. Ken held my hand and we walked by 21 pink recliner chairs, past 21 patients with IVs. At chair number 14 a nurse wiped a woman's brow with a damp cloth. The occupants of 17 and 18 stared at little T.V. screens suspended over their chairs. Some had people sitting with them while others sat alone, eyes closed.

We reached chair 22 in the far corner of the room. I sat down and took more deep breaths. A small woman of Philippine decent introduced herself as Winnie and explained the procedure to me. After confirming the proper prescription Winnie gave me six anti-nausea pills in three different colors. She sat close to me took my hand and asked, "Are you nervous?"

I couldn't speak. I nodded as tears threatened to spill again. Still holding my right hand she stroked my arm and told me to take a deep breath and relax. She spoke in a soft, soothing voice to calm me. I felt the liquid moving up my vein as the syringe pushed the drugs through the IV port in my arm.

"Drink lots of water over the next 48 hours," I was instructed. On a piece of paper the nurse wrote out my schedule for taking the anti-nausea pills. Once begun, the procedure took only thirty minutes or less. Then the waiting began. Waiting for reactions. *What will happen to me? How will I feel? Will I get sick? Will I get home before anything happens?*

That night the emotional strain of the day caught up with me. Upstairs, alone with Ken, I urgently needed a big hug. My rock of strength was there for me.

For three days after my chemo I felt sluggish and yucky but I never got sick to my stomach. I was pleasantly surprised since I expected the worst. By the fourth day I felt back to normal.

September 26, 1999

I left Chicago and Milwaukee behind me and began to relax as the congested traffic thinned out. Cities and towns gave way to dairy farms and pastures of grazing Holsteins. If only for a few days, I felt free again. The intense effort needed to cope with doctors, hospitals and healing was sidelined for a while. I had my Nikon camera on the seat next to me and I was excited about the possibility of capturing some good shots of the fall colors up in the Northwoods of Wisconsin.

Once I realized the worst was over, as far as my reactions to the chemotherapy, I got the OK from Dr. Hoffman to visit my parents and a dear family friend at her ranch in Marinette County. Ken was enrolled in a computer class at the local community college three days a week, so I drove the 4-1/2 hours alone.

Looking back on this trip, the photography metaphor became clear to me. For weeks my focal point had been an extreme close-up of my medical problems and recovery. The trip north was a redirection of focus, a change of lens. It was an opportunity to "zoom out" for a more inclusive view of life outside myself. The chance to combine some of my favorite things—horseback riding and being out in the midst of untarnished nature—in the company of very special people was a heavenly reprieve.

It had been an unusually mild and dry fall. The clear, sunny days stretched languorously on into November. During five of those perfect days the last week of September, I spent hours on horseback and on foot, exploring forests exploding with color. I filled my lungs with the crisp clear autumn air that carried the rich, earthy scents of the cyclical decay that is necessary for new growth come spring.

Bright yellow aspen trees standing next to fiery red maples vied for my attention; their falling leaves swirled like confetti in the wind. The flecks of color stuck in the boughs of the evergreens decorating them like ornaments on a Christmas tree. Orange and gold foliage covered the trail like a royal carpet beckoning me deeper into the woods. This was a joyous feast for my eyes. It soothed my soul and calmed my fears.

The trail twisted and turned as I continued on its uphill course until, finally, I arrived at Picnic Cliff on top of Thunder Mountain. There the vast sky reappeared as the oak and pine opened up to a panorama that took my breath away. It seemed as though I could see to the ends of the earth. The vision was much too grand to even attempt to photograph. I set my camera aside in order to experience the scene in a Zen sort of way, with an "in the moment" mindfulness that has a way of putting things back into proper perspective. I had been to this place before and seen the grand vista but it was as though I was seeing it anew, with different eyes. Everything was alive at that moment--the trees, the sky, the clouds, the rocks, the birds, the squirrels, the very air I was breathing. Everything was connected. Everything had a place and purpose, and I was part of it all.

Ironically, instead of feeling diminished and insignificant, I felt at peace and at one with the universe. My spirit soared. From that moment of moments I gathered the strength I needed to return to Chicago, where I would have to zoom in once again on my struggle against cancer. I felt confident that I could handle the challenges life tossed my way as long as I remembered to occasionally refocus on the big picture in order to keep my balance.

October 11, 1999

My oncologist warned me that my hair would fall out within three weeks of my first round of chemo. I would be bald. I couldn't imagine wearing a wig. Wigs—weren't they all big, ugly and obvious? Reluctantly, I decided to browse the wig shops while I still had hair. Maybe—hopefully—hair pieces had improved over the years.

I found a salon that specialized and marketed to women with hair loss due to chemotherapy. The stylists cut and shaped the wigs for a custom look. For fun I tried on long blond hair, bobbed black hair and wild red hair, but I ended up with a wig the color and style of my own hair. Contrary to what the movie star name suggests, my new Raquel Welch "do" was not glamorous or showy. My husband swore that my new wig looked natural. Even with Ken's reassurance that no one would notice, I was self-conscious. It felt funny, like I was wearing a hat.

Two days later my scalp began to hurt and my hair suddenly came out by the fistful. I expected it but it was nonetheless horrifying. Distressed, I told Fran, my mother-in-law, that I would rather shave my head than shed for days. When Ken returned from his computer class, he volunteered for the job. In the upstairs bathroom I sat on the toilet lid while Ken ran a razor over my scalp and recounted tales of his own drastic haircut when he entered the Air Force Basic Training years ago. Tears ran down my cheeks as my hair fell at my feet. *It's only temporary. It will grow back. It's not important*, I told myself. I dared to look in the mirror.

"I look like a Star Trek alien," I sobbed.

Ken held me and told me I was beautiful. *OK, that's enough crying. Get over it. There's more to you than your hair*, my alter ego lectured.

"Well, let's see," Fran called up from the living room.

I wiped my eyes, put on my baseball cap and went downstairs.

"You don't have to wear a hat here. Look, I knew it! You look good with that long neck of yours. You have a beautiful head."

Bless her! As I got used to seeing myself bald, I realized why it was so traumatic for me. I felt good and could trick myself into forgetting what I was going through—pretend I did not have cancer and that all was normal. There was no fooling myself anymore. One look in the mirror was an instant slap back to the reality of breast cancer. My smooth, shiny head and lack of eyebrows linked me to all those other souls in the pink recliner chairs in the chemo ward.

Maybe this was payback for all the times in my past when I noticed and commented on the shape of people's heads. My sister always thought it funny that when I described people I often mentioned their heads: "knife head" (very thin), "Charlie Brown head" (very big and round), "turtle head" (well, you can visualize it.) I had to laugh at myself. Now *my* head was exposed and naked for the entire world to see.

October 14, 1999

It was our sixteenth wedding anniversary. Ken and I had a date for dinner and a movie. Two days earlier I was given my second round of chemo, so I was not feeling 100%. I was determined to go out anyway. I got dressed up in a new outfit—black dress pants, black turtleneck sweater and a waist-length, gold, cashmere jacket. I even put on hair. It would be my first time I wore my wig in public. It itched and I was sure everyone would know it was fake.

Ken dropped me off at the door to the mall so I could check the movie times. A couple exited as I approached the door and I noticed that woman kept looking at me. *She's looking at my hair. She knows it's a wig.* When we got next to each other our eyes met and she spoke to me.

"You look terrific! That outfit is really sharp."

"Thank you," I said with surprise at the unexpected compliment. The woman was a perfect stranger but I wanted to hug her for making me feel so good in my moment of self-doubt. I couldn't get her out of my mind. *Was she another angel following me around to say just the right thing at just the right time to lift my spirit?*

November 1, 1999

I found myself sinking into a murky funk when my chemo dates approached. I hated going to the medical center. The treatment was as much a mental fight as it was physical. I wanted this nightmare to be over. I wanted to wake up on our sailboat in the warm, sunny tropics. As the temperature in Chicago dropped I thought of the island beaches graced with coconut palms. *Was it just a dream or did we really live that adventure?* On the days I struggled with the blues, I turned back to Nature. I walked, jogged and meditated by a nearby pond. I drew comfort from the breeze in my face, the ripple on the water and the rustle of the leaves in the trees. Regardless of what I endured, the world still turned. The sun rose and set, the moon shone in the night sky over Illinois just the same as in the islands. The awareness of that fact became my mooring line to sanity and allowed me to persevere another day. Each day brought me closer to cruising again.

Ken recorded another hypnosis tape for me, which helped me get through my last treatment calmly. For weeks I had envisioned a jubilant celebration following my last chemotherapy session. But as soon as we got out to the car in the medical center parking garage, I cried. *Why do I feel so afraid NOW? It is over.*

I felt confused and tired. Over the next several days I cried at the drop of a hat. My husband tried so hard to understand how I felt. I gave this some thought to try to figure it out. I hardly dared to verbalize my latest fear: *What if it comes back? How do they know if the cancer is completely gone?*

The next day I flipped through some pamphlets to read about the next round of fun: radiation. I came across a booklet titled "After Breast Cancer Treatment". On page one was a description of post-treatment stress—feelings of confusion, sadness and fear. Ironically, it said that women who cope best with treatments struggle with stress afterwards. Bingo!

OK, I'm not losing my mind. I can let the feelings pass and move on.

Chapter 15
Radiation

December 13, 1999

I was scheduled for thirty radiation treatments, arranged at the same time, five days a week. The two-day weekend gave my skin a little break. To avoid getting mired in Chicago commuter traffic every day for six weeks, I opted to go to a treatment center in the suburbs. I met with the radiologist, Dr. Awan, for a pre-exam and a briefing on the possible side effects: heart damage, lung scarring, and swollen arm. I fast-forwarded my brain through that wonderful information and focused on the fact that the radiation further reduced my chances of re-occurrence to 6%.

Next I was given a heart function test as a baseline, a cat scan, tiny tattoos to mark the target area, and had a mold made to hold me in the exact same position for each treatment. Ken accompanied me to my first treatment. It was fast and relatively easy. I marked of the visits on the calendar. *Only twenty-nine more to go.*

The daily drive through sleet and snow, to and from the radiation facility was trying. Preparing for holiday festivities helped to keep my mind occupied with pleasant thoughts. Christmas was especially wonderful for me. It had been several years since we had spent the holiday with my family at my parents home in Michigan. Family gatherings and traditions with loved ones seemed to be more important to me than ever. At Canadian Lakes the woods and fairways of the golf course were blanketed with snow. Inside a warm fire crackled. Sisters, spouses, nieces and nephews grandparents and grandkids talked excitedly to catch up with one another. We worked the jigsaw puzzle, built a snowman, played games, laughed at old family photos and ate nonstop. We all sat together at the candlelight Christmas Eve service at my parent's church. I was grateful to be there and as far as I was concerned, everything was perfect.

January 1, 2000

Ken and I rang in the New Year from the deck of the Abby, the ship that is home of the Columbia Yacht Club on Chicago's waterfront. It was an unforgettable spectacle of fireworks and an elegant and festive evening with all our boating buddies. Fatigue from my treatments was wearing on me but I managed to dance and celebrate a brand new year and life itself. New Years Day found me totally exhausted and zapped of energy.

January 4, 2000

Fifteen radiation treatments completed and fifteen more to go. I began to see the light at the end of the tunnel. By treatment number 20 my skin was red, burned and uncomfortable. My chest ached from radiation damage to the cartilage. I fought the fatigue and kept walking daily.

The act of walking kept my thoughts flowing. I became more and more philosophical and felt, as though I had reached an expanded or heightened awareness. I already had an appreciation for life but thoughts of my own mortality were not previously included in my thoughts. Now I faced those thoughts. It would take time to process all these new thoughts and feelings but I began to realize a new level of understanding of illness, pain and fear. I never went through a "Why Me?" stage. Somehow I got cancer and my job was to get through it and move on with my life. Suddenly, it seemed urgent for me to use my creative talents to express myself through art or writing or both.

January 15, 2000

Ken and I had planned to meet three other couples at a Spanish restaurant for dinner. As I stood in front of the mirror getting ready for our Saturday night date, I looked at my reflection. My hair was just beginning to grow back and I had a dark shadow of new growth that felt like Velcro over my formerly smooth baldhead. I put my wig on and fiddled with it. It made my head itch more than ever. I was still fussing with it when Ken came into the room and immediately sensed my faltering confidence.

"Forget the wig, Jane. Go without it. You look great," he urged.

I gave him a big hug. "Thanks. I love you for that!"

I looked back at my reflection. *Who am I wearing the wig for anyway? Is it for myself or for others so they aren't uncomfortable around me? Do I have the guts to go out to a restaurant on Saturday night? Can I handle the stares?*

I took a deep breath. *It's just not an important issue to dwell on. I can pull this off with attitude! Maybe I will give courage to another woman in the same situation who is afraid to be seen.*

At the restaurant I felt eyes on me as we walked to our table (or was it just my self conscious imagination?) My dear friends pretended not to notice my hairless head. But leave it to Ken to go straight to the obvious and ask, "So how do you like Jane's hair-do? Doesn't she look great?"

January 25, 2000

What a memorable day! My eyelashes are long enough to wear mascara once again and I completed my final radiation treatment-number 30. When Ken drove me back to the house there was a beautiful bouquet of flowers waiting from my true love and a bottle of champagne to celebrate the end of my treatments. I was finally finished! Now I could get excited about picking up life where I left off seven months ago. I could resume a "normal" life. I knew it would be weeks before I got my strength back but that was OK. I looked forward to naps and recuperation in the warm tropical sun.

I had a final visit with my oncologist who prescribed 20 mg of Tamoxifin daily for the next five years. I was given the green light to fly back to our sailboat in Panama. *Get me out of here!* I wanted to literally distance myself from the whole experience--as far away, as fast as possible. I wanted to wake up from the nightmare and pretend it never happened. Of course, that was impossible. A significant wind shift had occurred and the course of my life now flowed in a new direction. I could deny it or ignore it in my desire for normality, but the scars, fatigue and funky short hair would not let me forget. It would take months... years to digest and assimilate the internal emotional changes. But one thing was sure...I had a renewed appreciation for this gift of life.

Chapter 16
Return to Panama and the Rio Chagras

February 10, 2000

Ken and I flew from Chicago to Panama City, Panama. The next day we arranged for a driver to take us, along with our luggage and fresh provisions, across the isthmus to Jose Pobre Bay where we had left our sailboat seven months earlier. We found *Iniki* peacefully floating at anchor behind the mangroves at Marco's Marina. She was sound but very grubby from sitting without us since the previous July. All the fenders and lines were black and green. Inside, everything smelled moldy and rank.

Ken and I were so happy to be back to the boat but what a job we had ahead of us! It was difficult to decide where to begin the overwhelming cleanup. Ken started in the head, cleaning and opening valves while I tackled the refrigerator and freezer so we could store our fresh food. Next, I pulled out garbage bags and started filling them with purple pasta, bug infested beans, soggy cereal and scary looking stuff we could no longer identify. Sometime in November, one of Marco's helpers opened up *Iniki* to air things out. Apparently, he didn't dog down the hatches tight enough when he left. Later, during one of Panama's well known torrential downpours, rainwater seeped in under our settees where we stored all our canned goods. My photo albums, which I thought were safe in zip-lock bags, were also stored under the settees. I discovered three years of photos, over a thousand in all, were wet and ruined. I was heartbroken! For eight days we cleaned and repaired inside and out. I tired easily and had to stop many times to rest. But there was no complaint from me. It was a joy to be there working on the boat instead of sitting in a chemotherapy ward. Finally *Iniki* looked and smelled respectable again.

After we said our goodbyes to Marco we motored about six miles along the coastline to Portobelo. In its heyday Portobelo was the shipping point for all the gold and silver the Spanish plundered from South America. It is said that there was so much gold stored in the warehouses that the silver bars were simply piled in the street. We anchored under the protection of a high bluff with twelve ancient cannons from Fort San Fernando aimed down on us and decided we had earned a few days of rest and relaxation.

Our watermaker (reverse osmosis desalinator) wasn't working so after three windy days in Portobelo we headed for the Port of Cristobal and the nearby city of Colon to fix the problem. It was a downwind jib sail for three and a half hours.

February 23, 2000

Never in a million years did I ever dream that I would be sailing into Cristobal Harbor, the Caribbean entrance to the Panama Canal. But there I was, on our own sailboat, binocular in hand, searching for the sea buoy that marked the approach. Ken was at the helm, loving every minute of the experience.

Meanwhile, a container ship off our stern also approached the harbor entrance, rapidly closing the distance between us. The *Ever Delight* was an enormous vessel over three football fields in length, with a fresh coat of green paint and stacked high with shipping containers. From *Ever Delight's* bridge *Iniki* must have looked like a little toy bobbing on the water.

"Jane, get your camera. This is fantastic!" Ken exclaimed. It was usually my custom to snap photographs as we approached a new destination. But at that moment picture taking was not on my mind. I was a wee bit uneasy being so close to this maritime expressway where a steady parade of super-sized commercial ships came and went twenty-four hours a day. *Ever Delight* sounded one deep-toned blast of its deafening horn that resonated down on us from above like a warning from God Almighty! I nearly jumped out of my skin. The message was clear to me that we should get the heck out of the way. Ken calmly interpreted one blast to mean, "I am passing on your starboard side". No problem, no need to panic. We were not on a collision course. Just the same, I felt better when we started our engine, furled in our jib sail and fell off to show our clear intention to stay out of the way. Tonnage definitely rules.

Turbulence from the massive prop wash made the brown water ahead of us boil as we followed the colossal ship through the opening in the break wall, flanked by one hundred foot towers and proceeded on into the Port of Cristobal.

Inside the harbor massive red and green buoys guide the way to the Gatun Locks, the first of three sets of locks that raise and lower ships transiting the canal that connects the Caribbean Sea to the Pacific Ocean. Cristobal Harbor is three miles long and three miles wide, allowing plenty of room on either side of the channel for ships to anchor and wait their turn to enter the Panama Canal.

We counted twenty ships at anchor. One vessel we sailed by lay rusty and neglected, even stripped of its name and homeport, looking like a worn out old nag that was turned out to pasture with dim hopes of a future voyage. Tugboats sat at idle waiting for their next orders. Pilot boats buzzed around the harbor constantly picking up and dropping off the pilots that are required on every vessel going through the canal.

Yachts arriving in Cristobal Harbor either tie up at the Panama Yacht Club or must anchor in the F anchorage. We made our way to the "Flats" as the F anchorage is called and as the winds continued to blow like stink out of the northeast we set our hook into the muddy bottom. From there we had a wet dinghy ride into the Panama Yacht Club. All the guide books say that it is not safe to walk outside the yacht club fence. A 75 cent cab ride got us anywhere we needed to go in town.

Colon is a rough, tough, dirty, ugly, depressing, dilapidated, sweaty, infested miserable cesspool. I think that about covers it. Now that assessment is not just another privileged American's point of view. Colon has maintained its rough reputation for hundreds of years. Some fresh paint and some greenery and flowers would do wonders for the place. But unfortunately, crime is rampant and the dangers are real.

The cab drivers in Colon were nice and tried their best to accommodate their passengers. They were so eager for the fare that they always said they knew the place you wanted to go, even if they didn't. Then they would just drive around and hope to spot the place. We dropped off our laundry and were pleased to get it all back the next day. Ken found the parts he needed and fixed our watermaker himself.

The Panama Yacht Club was quite basic and functional with plenty of salty characters hanging around the docks and bar. The club served good food at very affordable prices. Everyone at the yacht club was waiting to transit the canal, working on their boat, provisioning for their next passage or leaving their boat there while they flew out of the country. Everyone had a story and nobody wanted to be there any longer than necessary. Ken and I were no exception.

When all our chores were accomplished we sailed twelve miles down the coast from Colon to the Chagras River. The Rio Chagras provides all the water for the Panama Canal. The electrical power generated by the Gatun Dam on the Chagras drives all the equipment involved in the operation of the Panama Canal, including the locomotives that tow the ships through the locks.

Fort San Lorenzo sits high on a bluff silently guarding the entrance to the Rio Chagras. After we zigzagged around a reef, a rock wash and sand spit and steered up the center of the river we knew we were in for a treat. Although the river was only a two-hour sail from Colon it was as if we had entered another time and dimension. We had entered the jungle, with all of its jungle noises and no evidence of human existence.

The sweet smell of flowers drifted through the air. The rainy season in Panama ended in January and in late February, a profusion of colorful and fragrant blossoms appeared everywhere. Iridescent blue butterflies fluttered erratically in the wind. The moving water glittered like diamonds and reflected the glaring afternoon sun back up to dapple the huge leaves along the banks. We loved it!

The river was fairly wide, deep and easy to navigate. We found a good spot to anchor about two miles up, just at a 90-degree bend in the river. There was a good breeze and a clear view in both directions to see any approaching boats.

With the anchor down we put up our awning before I sat down to listen to the symphony of sounds surrounding us.

I looked through the binoculars to get a better look at all the birds. Turkey vultures soared high in the sky. An osprey perched at the top of an open tree. There were herons galore, huge kingfishers, American swallow tail kites, hook-billed kites, tiny tree swallows swooping low over the water, large green parrots, and colorful toucans.

At dusk my eye caught a movement in the treetops very close to our boat. "Monkeys! A whole tree full of them!"

I could hardly contain my excitement as I passed the binoculars to Ken for a look. Black, medium sized with very long tails, they were busy eating blossoms or berries. Ken's fascination wore off pretty quickly but I watched for at least thirty minutes until the howler monkeys roamed from one tree to another away from the river to settle in for the night. Shortly after the sun went down a flurry of vampire bats appeared out of nowhere to feed on insects over the water. That was my cue to go inside. Bats give me the creeps and those were the biggest ones I have ever seen.

Early morning was a particularly rowdy time of day in the jungle. The howler monkeys enthusiastically announced the dawn. Their deep throated barking conjured up visions of tree climbing Rottweilers. Next, the parrots and toucans joined the chorus as the sun crept up over the canopy. They were pleasant sounds to wake up to.

During our time on the river Ken closely watched the weather for favorable conditions to continue sailing. While we waited for the winds that we wanted our days were a mix of boat maintenance and pleasure. We spent a few hours every morning on chores: changing the oil, lubing the winches, polishing the stainless steel. The afternoons were for fishing and exploring the many narrow creeks that meandered off the main river.

One afternoon we locked our dinghy to a pier near the mouth of the river and hiked about a mile up the jungle road to Fort San Lorenzo. As we got to a clearing near the fort we saw a very, very big black snake under some banana trees. It was the size of Ken's biceps and a good eight feet long. As soon as it sensed our presence it swiftly disappeared into the thick foliage. From that moment on, I was quite sure that I would not wander off the road without my snake boots and a big machete. On second thought, I won't go off the road at all!

The fort was like all the other forts in the Caribbean as far as I was concerned. They all look the same to me. However, the view from the ruins high on the bluff was magnificent and it gave us a chance to check out the state of the seas. The Caribbean was still quite lumpy with the winds out of the north to northeast at 25-30 knots. Since we wanted to sail north, we waited for the winds to clock around more to the east or southeast.

I didn't mind waiting for weather because I loved the jungle atmosphere on the river. I wondered if perhaps the earthy smells and the whole aura of the place touched some basic instincts still imprinted in our DNA or memories of a former primeval human existence. Maybe on some level deep in my soul I felt at home in the wild untamed forests. I thought of the tribes of people living in Panama and other jungles who still live exactly as their ancestors have for centuries with ancient knowledge passed down generation to generation, in perfect harmony with their environment. I gazed up at the same old stars in the night sky. Immersed in the blackness of that raw environment, worlds away from the pink recliner chairs, IV drips and high tech medical equipment, I recognized the call of the wild. I was strong enough to survive!

Three more sailboats came to explore the river. Each one found its own secluded spot. We couldn't see each other but we went by dinghy to meet them. Two boats were American and one was Swedish. We all kept our VHF radios on channel 72 to communicate if necessary. The Swedish couple spotted a 16-foot crocodile that swam up the center of the river in the middle of the day and managed to capture it on video. They stopped swimming in the Rio Chagras and so did we!

Chapter 17
Bocas del Toro to Guatemala

March 18, 2000

The little white-breasted bird was back again. It held a limp blossom in its beak as it perched on the ring where the topping lift connects to the end of the boom. It cocked its tiny round metallic blue head from side to side, wary and brave at the same time. When all seemed safe, it flew up under the sail cover and disappeared. A moment later it flew away, without the blossom.

For several days I waged a battle of wills with this persistent tree swallow. Regardless of the fact that there was literally a jungle full of trees and miles of river bank only yards away from *Iniki*, this determined nest builder was convinced that our folded, covered main sail was the perfect location for its forthcoming family.

I shooed it away. I knocked out the grass and twig deposits. I hoped the bird would give up and build elsewhere before things progressed to the point where eggs were laid. The vision of a nest full of cute fuzzy chicks falling to their doom next time we went sailing was a scenario I didn't want to be responsible for! Still, the focused bird would not be dissuaded from its mission. It simply started over again and again.

Now this got us wondering what else might be hiding in our sail. In the past month that we had been back aboard *Iniki* in Panama, our short trips from Jose Pobre Bay to Portobelo, to Colon, and to the Chagras River were all downwind jib sails. We had not yet raised the main sail. It was definitely time to examine it. Our calm anchorage in the Chagras River was an easy place to hoist the main and have a good look at everything.

As the sail unfolded dirt rained down on our clean deck (along with nesting material) Mud cocoons were stuck all over both sides of the sail. It was a regular nursery for mud-dabber wasps. It was hard to tell whether the larva was still in these things or already grown and gone.

Ken scrubbed a section at a time with a long handled brush and a bleach solution (no easy task when the sail hung limp and flopping) while I rinsed with the deck wash-down hose. When the critters build nests on your sails it is really time to go.

We looked at our options. Ken sat at the salon table with Chart 28006—South West Caribbean Sea spread out in front of him. The GPS was in his hand and the dividers, ruler and calculator were within reach. He studied the chart along with the most recent NOAA weather forecast for our area: south of 15 N and west of 80 W.

We wanted to go to San Andres Island 200 miles to the north but the winds were blowing out of the north. So Ken plotted our course from the Chagras River west to Bocas del Toro, Panama near the Costa Rican border. There is no protected anchorage along the coastline between the two points. The name of that area, Golfo de los Mosquitoes, is warning enough to stay offshore! It would be an overnight sail.

The following day at noon *Iniki* glided by the ruins of San Lorenzo fort for the second time. We left the murky brown Rio Chagras behind and were once again out in blue water. The barometer was holding steady at 1012, the winds were 18 knots from the northeast and we set a course of 270 degrees due west to Isla Escudo de Veragas near Bocas del Toro. The winds diminished throughout the day and by midnight we motored against strong currents with no wind at all.

The smell of freshly brewed coffee drifted out into the cockpit early next morning when Ken came out to take his three-hour shift. I saw him put out the fishing line with our faithful blue Rapella before I laid down to sleep. A few hours later I was up again as we neared our destination. We were approaching the island when suddenly the reel began to zzzzing as the 100 lb. test line flew out. The cry went out: 'Fish on the line!' Ken hauled in a nice 40" Wahoo. He quickly filleted it and put the line out again. In less than 15 minutes he was cleaning a second slightly smaller Wahoo. I cooked up fresh fish for lunch as soon as we got the anchor. There was enough fish in the freezer for several meals.

Isla Escudo de Veragas is home to a few lobster divers. They free dive-no tanks-to 60 feet to lasso lobsters live. A canoe stopped by our boat late in the afternoon to see if we wanted to buy lobster. Silly question! Fresh fish for lunch and fresh lobster for dinner---life is good.

Sometime after sundown the wind shifted and turned our peaceful anchorage into a rocking, rolling, jerk-you-all-around carnival ride. It made for a long night. I couldn't wait to pull up the hook the next morning.

We had a blissful easy day sail in a gentle breeze to Bahia Chiquiri. We spent two days at Zapatillo (slipper) Cay snorkeling and beach walking. This is a great cruising area with lots of places to explore as long as there is good light to read the water. It is a maze of islands, mangroves, shoals, and coral heads. We carefully eyeballed our way through narrow channels, past clapboard houses and tiendas built on stilts over the water.

Eventually we found our way to the 'coming back' town of Bocas del Toro, once home to the United Fruit Company and Chiquita Bananas. Tons of bananas are still exported from the area but the headquarters moved to the mainland. They say this dusty, rusty and peeling town is an up and coming tourist destination. It's quaint and charming in a rough-around-the-edges sort of way. Lots of young European backpackers have discovered it. Also, several Americans have built modest homes in the area since the dollar goes quite a bit farther there. Ken briefly considered the notion of settling down there after catching two fat 24" grouper fish from the dinghy with a hand-line. Our amazing blue Rapella came through again! (Or maybe it was my chanting and calling to the fish that did the trick). It was great fun and we were giggling like two kids who couldn't believe our luck. Too bad there wasn't anyone we knew around to show and tell.

March 28, 2000

We finally got the weather window we were waiting for to sail to San Andres Island. We had a pleasant and comfortable ride the whole way. The second morning in the faint pre-dawn light a pod of playful dolphins came along side the boat and entertained me with side flops, back flops and tail slaps. They seem to love to swim through the bubbles of the bow wake.

The water around San Andres was a beautiful ultramarine blue with incredible visibility. The depth gauge said there was 60 feet of water under our keel but we could clearly see the bottom. After 46 hours and 215 miles we arrived at the main town at the north end of the island. San Andres and its neighbor, Providencia, are both owned by Colombia. It is a safe and peaceful tourist destination with nice beaches, great restaurants, duty free shopping. The locals are quick to separate themselves from the troubled mainland.

We stayed for a week and then explored some little reef islands before sailing the 60 miles north to Isla Providencia. The sky turned shades of pink and peach in the fading light as we anchored under the outstretched arms of the Virgin Mary statue set high on the hillside of Catalina Harbor. Most of the residents of Providencia are proud descendants of the buccaneer Henry Morgan and a mix of European, Spanish, Indian and African blood. These good looking folks, who speak English, are quick to smile and offer any helpful services needed to make your stay a pleasant one.

While we were there Ken discovered an oil leak from the diesel and pinpointed it to the oil pressure-sending unit. It was a Saturday afternoon so many of the waterfront stores were closed. Ken didn't expect to find the exact part but he was hoping to get a brass plug to stop the leak until we could replace it. We walked up the road toward the airport to find an open hardware store. It was also closed but we were directed to the next store, which we were told, sold a bit of everything. They did not have what we needed but sent a man to walk us to a mechanic's house farther on down the road. After two or three more stops with no luck our escort waved at the passing vehicles and held up the part for them to see. Eventually, we were lead to a little shop on the side of a house with a cow in the back. Amazingly enough that man had what looked like a similar oil sending unit. We bought it, waved down a passing pickup and hitched a ride back to the town pier. As it turned out, the threads were wrong on the new part so it didn't fit.

But the search was an adventure in itself! Ken ended up plugging up the original with JB-weld to stop the leak and that did the job.

The next day was Palm Sunday. We heard there was to be a processional through town to the Catholic Church at 10 AM. It sounded like a great photo-op to me. I dug out a wrinkled skirt from the bottom of my closet, hoping that a splash of cologne would cover up the musty smell. There was a gathering crowd at the pier when Ken and I arrived. We were warmly greeted and handed hymn sheets printed in Spanish. Soon the priest showed up and donned his bright red robes, said something and sprinkled holy water on all the palm fronds before they were distributed. One kind woman made a special effort to get blessed palms for Ken and me.

The choir formed a line behind the priest and two alter boys while the rest of the group fell in line beside the choir. Ahead of the priest was a barefoot young "Jesus" with a painted on beard and brightly colored robe. He rode a reluctant, bony horse and led the palm waving procession along the coastline to the church as the choir sang loudly in two part harmony.

Even though it was Palm Sunday the Port Captain got our clearance papers all stamped and delivered to us later that afternoon so we could leave the following morning.

Once again, my weather guru, Captain Ken, picked a perfect weather window to leave Providencia. Our passage to the Bay Islands was over 400 miles-four days and three nights. We were able to sail the entire way with minimal seas and a big bright full moon each night to help with visibility. Many cruisers followed a shorter route that took them through the middle of a smattering of islands and shallow banks filled with unlit anchored fishing boats at the corner border of Nicaragua and Honduras. There was some recent pirate activity and cruisers shot and wounded while anchored at those islands. We did not want the anxiety of sailing through that mess so we took the long way up and over the top of the Gorda Banks away from all the hazards. We arrived safely in Guanaja, the eastern most island in the Bay Island group.

Exhausted swallow rests during our 4-day passage.

The only reason we wanted to stop in the Bay Islands was to find some old friends. In 1995 the 28 ft. Swedish boat, Tarona, sailed up to the dock of Columbia Yacht Club in Chicago. Pege and Marianne left Sweden three years earlier to sail around the world. They stayed at the club for a few weeks waiting for locks on the river to be repaired before they proceeded down the river system to the Gulf of Mexico. Ken and I got to be good friends with them during those weeks. We picked their brains about living on a sailboat and cruising full time because we had plans to do the same thing the following summer. We have kept in touch at Christmas every year since then. Marianne moved back to Sweden but she still goes to visit Pege a couple times a year. Pege was currently the caretaker of a lovely vacation home on the island of Roatan (Bay Islands). We had no way to let them know the time frame of when we would be sailing through. So we were especially lucky to be able to see both of them. We had such a fun time with them for two days before we moved on.

The sand flies were voracious in the Bay Islands which really put a damper on our desire to explore. I itched and scratched for days! We moved quickly from Roatan to Los Cochinos, to Utila. From Utila we had an overnight sail to the Rio Dulce in Guatemala—the hurricane hole for the Northwest Caribbean.

We checked into the country at the coastal town of Livingston at the mouth of the river. The next morning we began our trip up the river. For the first six miles the river snaked through a steep, jungley limestone canyon that was really quite dramatic. There were at least 20 canoes at the first curve with Indians net fishing for small baitfish. Birdcalls filled the treetops. Behind their melodious singing was a high shrill whine of insects that sounded like a ban saw cutting wood. Huts with steep thatched roofs were scattered along the riverbanks where the Mayan Indians continue to live the same life as their ancestors for centuries before them. White herons stood out against the lush greenery as they stalked fish along the banks. Cormorants were there one minute and gone the next as they dove underwater to catch fish.

The river widen into a lake, El Golfete. Farther inland it flowed into Guatemala's largest lake, Lago de Izabal. In between the two is the area where several marinas have opened up to accommodate the increasing number of foreign yachts seeking safe harbor for hurricane season.

We anchored there in one of the lagoons. The next day in our dinghy we took a look at a few different marinas and got a feel for the area. We got a slip at Bruno's Marina and left *Iniki* while we flew back to Chicago for Kassie's graduation ceremony from The Art Institute of Chicago. It was a two-day adventure just to get to the airport. We had the option of flying out of Guatemala City or Belize City. It was an all day bus ride from the Rio Dulce to either of those airports. It might have been easier to just sail *Iniki* all the way back to Florida! But then we would have missed a lot of beautiful sights.

Jane relaxing on bow in El Golfete

Chapter 18
The Rio Dulce and Antigua, Guatemala

October 2000

Water dripping on my face aroused me from some nonsensical dream. Abruptly awakened, I became aware that it was raining on me. I closed the hatch above the V-berth where we slept and glanced at my watch as I got up to close the other hatch and portholes.

It was 6:30 a.m. Standing in the companionway I breathed in the cool air. The smell of the fresh morning rain was delicious. I listened to the sound of the rain on the awning---the slow drops quickly increased to a pounding crescendo. I took another deep breath to savor the smell before making a pot of coffee. All too soon the sun would be sizzling once again. By 8 a.m., in the Rio Dulce during the rainy season, the heat and humidity take over, ruling the day, setting limits to our energy and activities.

The enticing aroma of brewing coffee roused Ken who got up and stretched. I handed him a steaming cup of "café con leche grande" along with a Mebendazole tablet. Two of those little pills daily for three consecutive days provided three months of protection from abdominal/intestinal parasite problems that are common in rural Guatemala. As the saying goes... "An ounce of prevention is worth a pound of cure."

That particular Tuesday in early October was scheduled to be a day of fun and sightseeing. Luckily the rain stopped and the gray clouds lingered all day providing us some relief from the scorching sun. According to plan, Ken and I went up to Bruno's Restaurant (an open air patio) at 7:30 a.m. to rendezvous with some folks from three other sailboats spending the 2000 hurricane season in the protected inland waters of the Rio Dulce. A total of nine people pitched in to hire a private, air-conditioned van with a driver for the equivalent of about $7.00 per person. One of the couples we met last winter in Panama. The others were new acquaintances. We were all eager to visit Quirigua (kee-ree-gwa) National Park and Mayan archeological site located southwest of the river. Although Quirigua was nowhere near the size of Tikal or Copan it had the best-preserved Stele in the Mayan kingdom.

We drove for nearly an hour to get there. Once off the main road we were bounced and jarred for a couple miles on a rough, muddy road that was lined with a 10-foot hibiscus hedge filled with crimson blossoms. Through the occasional gaps in the hedge I caught a glimpse of the neighboring banana plantation. Rows upon rows of trees heavy with large stalks of green bananas destined for export around the world.

We arrived at the park and paid our individual entrance fees of Q10. (At the time, the exchange rate was 7.6 Quetzales to $1.00 U.S.) It seemed as though the mosquitoes were hovering and just waiting for us to exit the van in anticipation of fresh blood. There was a simultaneous, synchronized scramble to unzip backpacks and grab the bug spray while swatting and fending off the buzzing little irritants. Once coated in deet the group split up to explore the ruins at their own pace.

Walking into the park I felt dwarfed by the massive ceiba trees along the wet stone walkway that led to the Grand Plaza of the site. There in the vast open grass clearing the towering carved stone steles stood like silent guards of the ancient civilization. The front and back of the stele usually showed a full-length portrait of the reigning king while the narrow sides held hieroglyphic text. These intricate details chiseled in rock 1500 years ago offer clues to the Mayan culture, its calendar, its rulers, battles, games and religious rituals for anyone clever enough to decipher their meaning.

I stood alone before one monolith over 38 feet tall. I gazed up at the elaborate feathered headdress, staff and shield so carefully rendered by this master craftsman. I was captured by the history and wonder of it all. *What stories were held there in stone? Who was King Jade Sky and what was the significance of the name Eighteen Rabbit?* These were real people lost and forgotten for a thousand years.

I was jolted out of my rumination and back into the 21st century by an unusual birdcall. Echoing from the canopy nearby, the cry sounded like a combination of a turkey gobble and a dove's coo. I spotted the yellow tailed bird with my binoculars near a cluster of hanging pendulum nests. I had to question a few people before I was told the bird was an oropendula.... not in my bird book.

I caught up with Ken who was having fun with his new digital camera. He took a photo of a worker sharpening his machete and was showing the image to the man as I approached. Imagine maintaining a lawn the size of three football fields with a machete! Two words come to mind: backache and blisters.

Beyond the plaza was a ball court for sports and ceremonial events and another structure being excavated. About 50% of the site is still buried. We walked around for over an hour then regrouped by the van.

Next we stopped to see a couple pueblos along the shore of Lake Izabal, the pretty 250 square mile lake that flows into the Rio Dulce. Izabal is a Mayan word meaning "where you sweat continuously". It is well named. We were grateful that the air conditioning in the van actually worked that afternoon.

After another week on the boat in the marina, the heat, humidity, daily rain and boredom threatened to drive me stir crazy. We felt trapped in the marina but we were paid through the end of the month. What we needed was another inland excursion. We did a little research, hired a van and went to Antigua and the highlands.

The drive from the Rio Dulce to Guatemala City was five hours. Even though the roads were good it is a difficult drive weaving through the mountains. I found Guate (Gwa-tay), as the capital city is called, unmemorable except for the choking haze of exhaust fumes from all the old buses and trucks that clog the busy streets.

After another hour of driving we arrived in Antigua. Dusk was settling in but it could not obscure the magical quality of the town. The buildings that lined the cobblestone streets were washed in earthy colors like mustard, moss and terra cotta with beautiful carved wooden doorways. Flowers graced the windowsills and Spanish style sconces blinked on to light the street corners. At the end of the street the surrounding mountains turned blue in the soft waning light. The crumbled stone ruins of once distinguished cathedrals and monasteries appeared every other block or so.

We found a wonderful place that was to be the base for our highland travels. Hotel Convent de Santa Catalina Martir, under the yellow clock tower arch on 5th avenue north was a convent built in the 1600's.

The rooms were off the tiled arcade that framed the courtyard. The nuns were no longer present but the serenity of the cloister remained. It was beautifully landscaped with large leafed plants crowding the corners and flowers hugging the flagstone walkways that crisscrossed to a central stone fountain adorned with potted geraniums. Ken was delighted to discover one of the rooms had been set up with several computers and Internet access.

We spent four days leisurely exploring on foot. Each morning we started the day with an early breakfast at our favorite spot, Café Condessa just off the main town square. There they served great coffee and fresh warm scones with "creme fresca" next to a bubbling fountain in yet another lovely courtyard with 500-year-old walls.

Clocktower Arch, Antigua, Guatemala

Woman selling tortillas & beans, Antigua

Small girl selling newspapers, Antigua

Mayan women in Antigua

Gardener at our hotel, Antigua

One of many interesting doorway, Antigua

Antigua was once the capital of Guatemala so there were many grand government buildings along with numerous churches and fine aristocratic homes. There were so many earthquakes, volcanic eruptions, and mud slides in the city's history that the capital was moved to Guatemala City. However, the citizens of Antigua have meticulously maintained its colonial charm, which is its appeal to the tourists who flock there, national as well as, foreign. Many wealthy Guatemalans flee the capital city on the weekends to enjoy the many fine restaurants and wonderful ambiance that Antigua offers. There were over 50 language schools in operation, so there were many students of all ages learning Spanish.

The Central Plaza was the heart of the city. Around the grand Fountain of Sirens park benches under big old shade trees provided a cool place to observe the action and visit with friends. A large congregation of venders loitered around waiting for targets like us. Men and boys sold imitation jade necklaces, wooden masks and flutes. Mayan woman in their colorful outfits walked around with a stack of their woven cloths for sale balanced on their heads. These were plucky, persistent women. Many had babies wrapped up on their backs or tiny miniatures of themselves hanging onto their skirts.

The women were not easily brushed off. They had a comeback for every objection and some even knew some key English phrases: "Special price for you. You buy, you husband pay. Buy for your mother. Buy for your sister. You buy for Christmas. I have other colors, other sizes. OK, how much you pay?"

Most women had a good sense of humor and laughed at Ken's teasing and joking. But one must have been having a bad day and called him an "elbow". We later found out that when they point to their elbow, the gesture means you are cheap! But bargaining was all part of the game and was expected.

I shot rolls and rolls of film. Everything caught my eye...donkeys loaded down with firewood, small bronze-skinned men pushing and pulling large loaded down wooden carts, small children selling newspapers and shoe shines, woman selling their homemade tacos in the street, volcanoes shrouded in clouds, church bell towers, the flower market and fruit stand and the brightly painted chicken buses with their dashboard full of religious symbols and little statues to protect them on the trip.

Wherever we went it seemed like church bells were constantly ringing. They rang all around the town on the hour and quarter hours. The monasteries and convent also rang before and after the hours, as a signal to prayers. Sometimes the bells rang in double time. Often firecrackers were set off on the church steps to call the spirits. In the 16th and 17th century Antigua had 38 churches and 16 religious orders. The bells must have been deafening.

Weaver with a back-strap loom

Weaver & daughter at artisan shop

Sampling the local brew

Chapter 19
The Highlands of Guatemala

October 15, 2000

There were 6 more weeks of hurricane season before we could take *Iniki* out of the Rio Dulce and safely sail the waters of the Caribbean Sea once again. We had time to get off the boat and take another trip inland. Ken and I decided to visit the Central Highlands of Guatemala. We thoroughly enjoyed Antigua and wanted to explore further into the mountains to see how the Mayans lived. We also wanted to explore the area around Lake Atitlan, reputed to be the most beautiful lake in the world.

We took a van from Antigua to Lake Atitlan, a two hour ride through mountains and valleys that were beautiful beyond words. One wide valley was divided up into plots growing corn, cabbages, potatoes, and beans in perfect hand tilled rows. I smelled the pungent aroma of onions, and then around the bend came the sweet smell of melons. In some places one or two men worked a plot. In other places the whole village came together to bundle and tie onions or fill sacks of potatoes.

The road climbed higher. The cultivated plots shrunk and blended together like patchwork pieces of a grand fertile quilt—with a variety of patterns, shapes and texture. A well-worn footpath followed the twists and turns of the paved road we were on. Cows and sheep grazed tied to short tethers. A boy walked a pig on a rope. A bent over man with a weathered face carried a heavy load in a bundle on his back, supported with a leather strap around his forehead. I gave up counting the missed photo-ops as our van whizzed on by.

We literally drove on up into the clouds and were soon engulfed in fog and mist for a while. When it cleared and Lake Atitlan finally came into view I was dumbfounded by the spectacular site of the shimmering blue water at the base of three volcanoes. Several more descending hairpin turns brought us down to the northeast shore and the town called Panajachel (pana-ha-shell) where we spent the night.

Mayan man in highlands of Guatemala

Headdress demo in Panajachel

Mayan backpack

We had a chance to walk around before dark and worked out a plan to see some of the traditional Mayan villages around the lake. We found a ferryboat that visited three of them in one day so we signed up to go with them early the next morning.

It was an hour ride across the calm flat lake which was actually a great volcanic crater filled with water. It is so deep they have not found the bottom in some places. The three volcanoes that majestically framed Lake Atitlan were reflected in the glassy surface. By mid-afternoon everyday the winds piped up creating a stiff chop and made for a chilly return trip. The volcanic slopes provide the Mayans nutrient rich soil for growing crops but the angle was so steep in some places the men had to secure themselves to a tree as they worked to keep from tumbling to their doom.

When Ken and I began our inland travels around Guatemala we were excited to see a way of life so foreign from our own. Seeing the Mayan women in the cities dressed in their vibrant huipils (hand woven blouses), wrap skirts and headdresses selling their wares to tourists was a curiosity. To see them kneel on the ground weaving intricate high quality designs by hand with simple looms secured around their middle with a leather strap while the other end was tied to a tree or pole was a marvel.

As we wandered higher into the small mountain villages we began to see things with a different set of eyes--with a desire to look deeper for a better understanding. At first glance one might be tempted to say the Mayan lifestyle is simple and primitive.

The Mayan lifestyle is indeed ancient but it is complex. From what we read about the Mayan people and discovered first hand, we found wisdom and a philosophy of life that just might add a little balance and contentment if incorporated into our fast paced, high tech society.

All three villages that we visited around Lake Atitlan were situated high above the shoreline so it was quite a workout hiking up the very steep cobblestone streets. The second village at the south end of the lake at the base of the volcanoes was called Santiago Atitlan.

Santiago Atitlan was home and the center of the universe for the Tzutujil Mayan people. There is no word in their language for leaving. No matter where they are going, no matter how long, they are always returning home. There is no place else they would rather be. That particular village is desperately clinging to its traditional language and clothing. It is said that once the language and clothing are given up the people cease to be Mayan and become Guatemalan. The rich culture is lost. It is a tragic saga of indigenous people around the world that saddens my heart.

Today, there on the shore of the beautiful mountain lake, the Tzutujil village continues to have a reputation of stubborn resistance. There was much pressure to change their ways from political and religious powers. Consequently, the "death squads" targeted the village, along with many others in the 1980's and thousands of Mayan people were killed in Santiago Atitlan. The village was also interesting because of its reverence for Maximon (mah-shee-mohn) a local deity who is a blend of ancient Mayan gods, Judas Iscariot, and Pedro de Alvarado, a bold conquistador of Guatemala. His effigy is a wooden mask with a black hat, a big cigar and colorful scarves. Maximon resides in a different house every year, which is considered a great honor. Offerings of candles, beer, liquor and money are brought to him to ensure health, protection or forgiveness.

As soon as our boat arrived at the village and we stepped out onto the dock a man offered to guide us to the market, church and Maximon. We didn't need a guide to find the market or the church but we were very curious to see the Maximon shrine. I noticed that the man was not wearing the customary clothing style of the village. Obviously he was cashing in on showing traditionalist rituals to the tourists, so I wondered about the authenticity of what we would see. Always the negotiator, Ken worked out a deal with him and off we went.

We climbed the steep road to the village center. It just happened to be their big market day of the week. Trucks loaded with people from other villages, noted by their different colored huipils, arrived to trade goods around the square. The women sat on the ground with their legs folded under them in their long skirts, surrounded by woven baskets or plastic bowls full of various items for sale. There were vegetables, spices, honey, eggs, live chickens and homemade chocolate, with or without sugar. The street was a riot of color. The men gathered in small groups off to the side conversing in their striped knee pants tied with woven sashes around the waist. They also all wore leather or rope sandals and black felt or white straw cowboy hats.

Chickens for sale

Vegetable market

Maximon

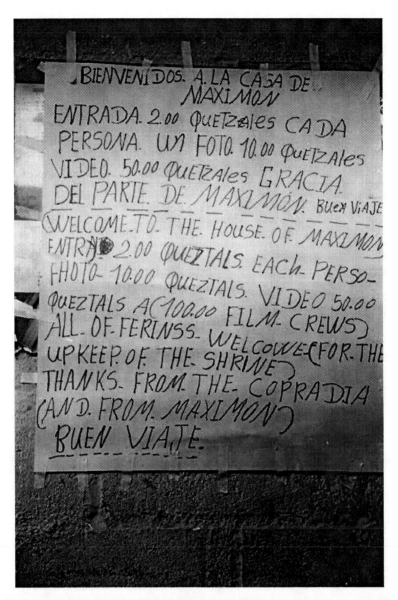

Rules to see Maximon

Traditional wear in the Guatemalan highlands

Headdress from Lake Atitlan area

Our guide, Ramón, told us that Maximon was a little bit further uphill. We followed him as he turned off the cobblestone street onto a footpath between living compounds divided into family groups. Each of those compounds, some bigger than others, consisted of a cooking hut, an animal pen, family gathering place, sleeping huts for parents, other sleeping huts for married children and their families.

The Maximon shrine was in one such compound. A hand written sign in English and Spanish spelled out the rules of the visit. The fee was 2 Quetzals (about $.20 US) to visit, 10 Q ($1.50 US) to take one photo, and 50Q ($7.00 US) for a video. The cash was payable to Maximon.

We were led through a curtained doorway. It took a moment for our eyes to adjust to the small dark candle lit room. The stuffy closeness was intensified by the smoke and smell of burning incense. In the center of the room was Maximon. A man attending to him took the cigar out of Maximon's wooden mouth and proceeded to pour some rum into the mouth, careful to wipe any drips with a cloth before replacing the cigar. There were women seated on benches along the back wall. On either side were decorated carved figures like the ones seen in the churches.

Standing in front of Maximon was a man who, we were told later, was ill and had come to be healed. With his eyes closed and eyelids fluttering, Ken could see that the man was in a trance state. The shaman healer was chanting, lighting candles, swinging incense and directing the smoke around the sick man's head.

We watched in silent fascination for several minutes. Then Ramón told us, in so many words, that it was time to pay up and take the photo. Ken put the money in the collection plate by the beer bottles and candles on the floor in front of Maximon. I hoped my one shot would be a good one, knowing full well it could not possibly capture the essence of the experience. The shaman ignored us and kept on chanting and gesturing. Ken was captivated. He would have stayed for hours but I couldn't breathe and our guide was ready to go.

Everyone in the village seemed to know our guide Ramón. Everyone spoke to him as we passed. On our way back downhill Ramón took a string of antique jade beads out of his pocket to show us and asked Ken if he was interested in them. Ken had seen some similar long hollow beads in South America and knew they were very valuable. Ken asked Ramón if he could scratch one of the beads with his knife. (Real jade will not scratch.) This was the genuine article, perhaps hundreds of years old. Ramón wanted $20 U.S. dollars for the beads and Ken happily agreed.

Ramón eagerly led us to his house. The small room had a dirt floor, one low wooden stool, a hammock and a small black and white TV. Out a back door and down a few dirt steps three women were kneeling on a mat on the ground weaving. When they saw us they quickly stopped what they were doing and brought their cloths to us while Ramón found some wooden carvings and pottery to show. We didn't buy anything more but thanked him just the same for taking us to his home.

The trek back to the launch was interrupted many times when women put their scarves and things over my shoulder wanting us to buy, buy, BUY! Little girls trailed us holding up bracelets, refrigerator magnets and whistles. Their imploring big brown eyes were hard to refuse. I have a lifetime supply of woven bracelets and peeper-keepers! We thought the boat would be a safe refuge but they followed us right on board, sat down all around us and kept up the pressure.

After an identical high pressure selling experience in the third village we were most anxious to retreat to some private space for the remainder of the afternoon. The next day we were in a van on the way to Chichicastenango to see the well-known Sunday market. From Antigua we made arrangements to travel further into the highlands.

Chapter 20
Tikal

November 2000

We continued our travels in the Guatemala highlands while our sailboat, *Iniki*, awaited our return in the Rio Dulce. From Lake Atitlan, Guatemala we boarded a van with five other people and traveled for about an hour to get to the village of Chichicastenango, which means the place of the Chichicaste. Chichicaste is a plant like nettles. Tenango means "the place of".

Chichicastenango is the place of the nettles.

Along the way we drove through a valley of apple orchards and saw bushels of red apples for sale along the roadside. Soon we were winding through mountains that were covered with tall virgin pine forests. The air smelled heavenly. Chichicastenango is perched on a mountaintop at an altitude of 6000 feet. We arrived just as the sun was setting.

We made a point to go to Chichi, as it is called for short, on Saturday and spend the night so we could see the famous Sunday Market—one of the biggest in the highlands. It was also our seventeenth wedding anniversary so we splurged a little on a room (relatively speaking for Guatemala—we paid $60 instead of the usual $25 or $30)

We checked in to the Mayan Inn located just a few steps from the market area and Santo Tomas Cathedral. The small reception office provided no clue to how lovely the inner sanctums and rooms of the former monastery were.

There are no locks on the doors and therefore, no keys. When we were taken to our room we were given a printed card that read:

"Your Right Hand Man -Jorge Pol Canil

He is your Waiter and Room Attendant. He is held responsible

for the complete inventory of your room and must check to see

that you do not leave any of your personal belongings behind."

I suddenly envisioned a scenario where I mindlessly left my toothbrush behind resulting in Jorge's demise at a sacrificial altar!

Our room was charming. The bed's antique headboard was hand carved and painted with a pastoral scene. We were told it once belonged to the Bishop of the monastery. There was a little fireplace all set with a neat stack of extra wood and fresh flowers on the mantle.

Jorge managed to turn down our bed, light the fire and a few candles in our room before we returned from the dining room where he had just served us dinner. The fresh mountain air was a nice change from the sweltering heat of the river basin where our sailboat was docked.

Jorge Pol Canil, Chichicastenango

Before dinner we took a stroll around the streets to get our bearings. Local people from the surrounding villages arrived carrying bamboo poles to set up their booths and spend the night in preparation for the market the next morning. Twice a week, on Thursdays and Sundays these ambitious souls walked up and down steep rough roads to get to the market, set up their booth, then broke it down and walked back to their home --which could be miles away. It was not an easy life. But it seemed to be an enjoyed social gathering.

I noticed that they don't set out just a few samples, which would facilitate setup and breakdown. No, if they sold wooden masks they hung up 100 masks. If they sold woven cloth, they hung up 200, many identical. Ceramic water pitchers were stacked in great mounds and so on. This must have somehow been significant in distinguishing a good merchant in their eyes.

The first mortar launched rocket exploded with a loud boom at 6 a.m. Sunday morning. By 6:30 a.m. Ken and I were making our way to Santo Tomas church where more mortar rockets were being launched from the giant sized stone steps. Children watched and put their fingers in their ears waiting for the next explosion.

Santo Tomas cathedral was built on top of a sacred Mayan Temple site (another attempt at repression). But the ancient rituals continue on the church steps just as they were done in another era on the steps of the Mayan Temple. Families left offerings of flower petals, incense and corn and said prayers before ever entering the church.

It seemed like we had entered some medieval time warp. We watched a Mayan shaman as he lit candles and swung a can of incense at the front entrance. He sprinkled liquor on the door and spread flower petals outside and inside the doorway. On an altar at the base of the steps the shaman meticulously laid an arrangement of bark, moss, incense sticks, cigars, candles in different significant colors and flower petals.

I tried to be inconspicuous as I took pictures with my zoom lens. But apparently I got too close and the holy man showed his displeasure by throwing and hitting me with a piece of bark! *OOPS*. I backed off and lowered my camera as he proceeded to light and burn the offerings.

The Cofradias (Brotherhood)

Jane Grossman

Mayan alter on church steps

Shaman sets up alter

Mayan Shaman performs rituals

Mayan rituals in Chichicastenango

The brotherhood chant facing four directions

A steady stream of men and women arrived carrying heavy loads to their stalls. Small children followed their parents carrying bundles sized accordingly. I stood in one place out of the way and scanned the crowd. An old wrinkled woman sold bunches of long stemmed calla lilies, a young woman walked by with a basket full of peeping fuzzy yellow chicks balanced on her head while her

179

arm was through the handle of a soft basket containing a live turkey with its red knobby head sticking out the top.

Turkeys for sale

That's when we heard the live music. We looked in the direction of the sound and saw a procession approaching the cathedral. Men playing a drum, a wooden flute and horn led the group. There was really no discernible melody that I could hear and concluded it was just more noise to add to the fireworks.

Following the "musicians" were the cofradias or brotherhood of the village. There were six of them dressed in black knee pants and short black jackets covered with gorgeous embroidery. Red woven scarves were wrapped around their heads with long tassels hanging down their backs. They each carried a long staff and climbed two by two up the church steps to the front entrance. Before the doors where the shaman had previously left offerings, the brotherhood knelt down on one knee as they chanted prayers aloud. Prayers were chanted in each direction: north, south, east and west. Then they walked single file in a small circle a couple times, still chanting, before proceeding into the old church.

Overhead the clouds parted. Rays of light from the rising sun shone through the lacy metal cross on top of the bell tower illuminating the swirling incense smoke that shrouded the front of the church creating an eerie, mystical setting to the scene unfolding on the steps of Santo Tomas that Sunday morning. We wandered through the market and picked up a few small trinkets. I bought the bundle of wood pieces required to put together a back strap loom. If I can ever figure out how to set it up I will try my hand at weaving.

Our van collected us later that afternoon and we returned to Antigua. Two days later we were on our boat again in the Rio Dulce. We slipped back into our on-board routine for another week. But there was still one more place we wanted to visit before we left Guatemala. We had to see the ancient Mayan temples of Tikal.

Carrying just one backpack each, plus my camera, we boarded the big modern Linea Dorado bus and traveled north from the river to the town of Flores on Peten Itza Lake. It was a comfortable 3.5-hour ride in nice reclining seats. We made a few undesignated stops at houses that seemed to be in the middle of nowhere. Whole families emerged to happily greet the bus driver who handed over bags of groceries and large cans of powdered milk. Perhaps they were relatives.

The bus was too big for the narrow streets of the town of Flores so we were transferred to a mini van and delivered to the lodging of our choice. This shuttle service was called Mundo Maya and the driver agreed to return for us at 8 am the next morning to drive us to Tikal. Ken and I had an early breakfast so we'd be ready and waiting for our ride. Eight o'clock came and went. Typical. At 8:20 a van pulled up and stopped. The driver looked at us and said, "Tikal?"

I held up my ticket receipt and asked in Spanish, "Mundo Maya to Tikal?"

"Si, Si" –yes, he replied. So we climbed in the van.

At another hotel in town we picked up two Frenchmen who smelled so bad I had to cover my nose to breathe. The next stop was the small airport where a guy with more authority asked to see our voucher. He chewed out the driver and told us we were in the wrong van. I tried to explain that we had probably missed the correct van now because of the mistake and suggested that we just continue on with this van.

"No, can't do that. It is a different company."

So back we went to town and the Mundo Maya office. I had my head out the window like a dog biting the air for relief from the stench of body odor. *How can someone smell so bad so early in the day?* At the office more incompetence was in action. The employee would not pay the other company to drive us, nor would she refund our fare so we could pay the other company to drive us. Our go-with-the-flow and roll-with-the-punches travel attitude was quickly dissolving. The "wrong" driver gave up, left us there and drove off with the two hygienically challenged Frenchmen. For twenty minutes we waited for the boss to show up while the employee pretended to be very busy. A simple phone call from the manager, once she arrived, summoned another van to take us to Tikal. We only had to pull over to the side of the road twice so the driver could tighten the front wheel onto the axle. It was a little disconcerting.

It was 11:00 a.m. by the time we finally arrived at the Tikal Visitors Information Center. Ken and I agreed that we would get much more out of the visit with a knowledgeable guide. It proved to be a good decision. Noah was about 25 years old and spoke excellent English. He told us he spent five years in Belize learning the language and another 3 years of study and exams to become a licensed tour guide. He really knew his stuff. We followed Noah down jungle paths that connected the different building complexes of the park and avoided the crowds on the main roadways. We saw monkeys in the treetops and stepped over farmer ant thoroughfares that crossed our path. There were many sites that remained unexcavated. Large trees grew out of overgrown pyramids and altars lay trapped on the ground under a tangle of serpentine roots. We could easily imagine how Tikal looked to the first chicleros (gatherers of chicle) who stumbled on the abandoned and forgotten city.

Coatimundis, a funny looking cousin of the raccoon, waddled around all over the park with their long tails straight up in the air, long snouts sniffing and looking for hand outs from the visitors. A gray fox trotted out from behind a tomb unconcerned with our presence. A small flock of beautiful Ocellated turkeys pecked in the grass but were more wary of humans than the other critters.

Noah spoon-fed us just the right amount of information to hold our interest without overwhelming us with too many dates. He had a flare for drama in his presentation the way he led us up the backside of the acropolis on the Grand Plaza. At just the right moment he stopped talking, took us around a moss-covered corner to reveal the splendid full view of the city center. Temple I and II rose like majestic mountains before us on the east and west end of the plaza. The immense scale was even more apparent looking down on the Lilliputian tourists walking on the lawn below and struggling to climb the steep temple steps. When we got down to ground level to look around there was a large group of Mayan Indians gathered on the lawn burning incense. The site is sacred and they visit often to honor the gods and ancestors with offerings. The ritual will insure a season of good crops.

Tikal means the "Place of the Voices". I could almost hear them. The sight of the people in traditional dress among the grandeur of the temples fueled my imagination. In my mind I saw King Ahow Cacau draped in jaguar skins and brilliant feathers; priests adorned in jade in a cloud of smoke as they chanted prayers to Chaoc, the rain god, in the shadow of the towering Temple of Masks. There were strong vibes there!

The top of the Temple of Inscriptions or Temple IV was a popular place for tourists to watch the sunrise. Wooden stairs with handrails were built up the backside of the overgrown structure. One look at those stairs and I couldn't imagine climbing them in the dark before dawn. Ken had no desire to go up even in the daylight but Noah promised me a great view. So I climbed the gazillion steps to the top by myself -- 230 feet above the ground. My heart was pounding and my thighs were shaking when I reached the top. But oh, what a sight! It was the view of a soaring eagle. I was above the forest canopy and the tops of the ancient temples rose up out of the sea of green that stretched for miles. Exotic sounds echoed from the jungle below. I sat down on the 1500 year old steps to take it all in and marveled at the architectural triumphs accomplished without the help of modern technology.

Mayan Temple, Tikal

View from the top of Temple IV, Tikal

Once we got back to the Rio Dulce we worked hard to get *Iniki* ready to leave the river. We put our cleaned and restitched sails back on, changed the oil, and patched the leaks in our tired dinghy. The hull was buffed and waxed. Ken rebuilt the head and replaced all its parts—a grueling eight-hour job. Never underestimate the joy of a working toilet!

Ken rebuilds the head

One afternoon we were walking through the little town by the river spending the rest of our Guatemalan money before leaving. We just bought some vegetables and fruit from the street venders when Ken spotted a man with a guitar standing around next to a stall.

"How much to play a romantic song for my wife?" Ken asked him in Spanish.

"Ten Q" he answered.

Ken held out two coins and said, "I only have 2Q. Can you play her a short one?" Two Quetzals is the equivalent of about 26 cents. I smiled with delight that my husband thought of the idea, and the musician agreed to play. He asked where we were from and did I want to hear an American song?

"No, Senior. I want to hear a love song from Guatemala."

That must have pleased him because for 26 cents he sang a long song with several verses. He had a beautiful strong voice and quickly drew a crowd in the street. I loved it!

Besides being anxious to sail, swim and fish again there was another reason we were in a hurry to leave as soon as we were sure hurricane season was really over. Security on the river became a serious problem. When we arrived we were warned to keep things locked up, but that was standard procedure for us ever since we left Chicago. There were reports of boats getting broken into and robbed after dark when the people left to go ashore. By October and November the armed robberies after dark increased to 2 or 3 a week and even occurred on occupied boats. It was like the wild, wild west! It wasn't just the boaters who were hit. The local stores and gas stations were robbed too. Even the Coca-Cola delivery trucks had guards with shotguns riding the rear.

The Port Captain held onto boater's weapons during their stay in the country and the bad guys knew it. Just before we left a single-hander was boarded and robbed at gunpoint while he was underway down the river.... in broad daylight! Boaters began hiring armed guards and traveled in flotillas to get safely back to the mouth of the river and out to sea.

On our trip down the river we were especially cautious in the Golfete area where the river widened into a lake. That's where several ambushes occurred. As we motored *Iniki* through that danger zone on high alert, a large local canoe with a big engine and four or five men left one side of the river and headed right for us. Ken aimed a loaded flare gun on them---it was a straight-armed, I'm-not-messing-around stance. They crossed right in front of our bow. Their eyes were wide and their jaws dropped at the sight of Ken ready to shoot and they kept on going at top speed to the opposite shore. They may have been completely innocent but maybe not. We'll never know. We made it safely to Livingston at the mouth of the river. When we checked out the Port Captain handed over our Mossburg along with our stamped exit papers. As we walked back to the pier no one blinked an eye at Ken carrying a 12-gauge shotgun through town. We were ready to leave Guatemala in the morning.

Checking out of Guatemala

"Evil eye" to discourage thieves on our boat

Chapter 21
Belize

November 16, 2000

At high tide on Thursday morning *Iniki* skimmed over the sand bar at the mouth of the Rio Dulce. At long last we cruised out of Guatemala where we had been for 5 months awaiting the end of Hurricane Season 2000. We turned *Iniki* northbound and headed for Punta Gorda, the first port with Customs officials on the mainland of Belize. The sea was flat with very little wind so we motored along at 6 knots feeling lucky to get out of Guatemala unscathed...or so we thought. As much as we loved our travels in Guatemala we were ready to get away from the dangers.... specifically, the armed robberies, the weekly bus crashes killing 60 people at a time and tropical diseases!

We arrived around 1:00 pm and anchored off the end of the pier. All of the officials we were required to see had their offices in the same building at the end of the dock. The fact that Belize is the only English speaking country in Central America also facilitated our check in procedure. We used our brand new 2 horsepower Yamaha to putt-putt our dinghy to shore. Our 9.9 hp Honda outboard was giving us problems and was very unreliable. So we bought the little Yamaha in Guatemala as a back up.

I think the Port Captain was bored that day since he wanted to go out to personally inspect our boat and "seal" our weapon in a locked lazerette. The Quarantine/ Agricultural man came along as well to look at our fruits and vegetables. By the time we returned the men to shore, collected our paperwork and picked up a few items at the grocery store, the afternoon was slipping away. We needed to get underway to find a better overnight anchorage. Moho Cayes, a small group of islands 6 nautical miles away was our destination for the night. It would take us over an hour to get there and we had just about that much daylight left.

Half way there Ken was at the helm when a local boat came speeding into view. There were several people aboard dressed in black and it was heading straight at us. With all the armed boardings in Guatemala and Honduras still fresh in our minds, Ken told me to get the flare guns. Ken wasn't aiming the flare gun at them but it was loaded and down at his side. The launch kept on coming at us. I grabbed the binoculars for a better look at these guys. I saw people in diving gear, fancy straw hats and fishing poles! (Local fishermen use nets or hand lines.) When they got within 50 yards they yelled and waved as some of them snapped photos of our boat. They were just a happy bunch of tourists, obviously having a good ol' time returning from an afternoon dive out on the reef. Ken and I laughed in relief. It sure was nice to be in friendly Belize!

The sun melted into the mountains on the mainland behind us, spreading puddles of color that were soaked up by the cotton ball clouds. It was unusual for us to be arriving at a new place without good light to read the water. I was on the bow straining to see the coral heads and shallow spots in the fading light as we moved ahead slowly toward the island where we wanted to anchor. The water was getting thin. The depth gauge read 4.6 feet when *Iniki* touched bottom and came to a halt.

I was worried about it getting dark but Ken said the tide was on the rise so he wasn't overly concerned. On deck we carried twelve 5-gallon jerry cans with extra diesel, gasoline and water. They had all been filled just before we left the Rio Dulce. So when Ken couldn't bully us off with the engine his first thought was to unload the jerry cans into the dinghy. That was almost 500 pounds we could get easily off the boat. Ken handed the twelve containers down to me in the dinghy. When he put *Iniki* in reverse she floated right off the shoal. I scrambled back aboard and we found our way to 13 feet of water to set the anchor for the night, vowing not to cut it so close next time.

That evening Ken was not feeling well and complained of bad headache. He proceeded to plot our course for the next day on the charts and programmed the waypoints into the GPS.

"Why am I so sore from head to toe?" he wondered aloud.

Ken stretched out on the settee and went right to sleep. I woke up in the middle of the night and found him shivering. He was freezing and couldn't stop his teeth from chattering, yet he was burning up with fever. I dug out some extra covers to warm him up. By morning his temperature came down a bit but was still 101 degrees.

With Ken not feeling well we would normally have stayed put and not moved the boat. But a cold front was coming down from the north and we needed better protection from strong north winds. Before he got sick we planned to meet some friends at the Sapodilla Cays, the southern most group of islands on Belize's outer reef. We stuck to that plan since we hadn't yet figured out what Ken had and hoped it was just some 24-hour bug. Ken helped get the anchor up and set the sails but once we got underway and on course he went below to lie down with a cold compress on his head. The sky was cloudy to match my overcast state of mind. I was worried about Ken. He's rarely sick and this thing hit him hard. I started to wonder if it was malaria because of the high fever. If it really was malaria we had medication for it on board.

I motor-sailed east past Lawrence Rock and through the break in the reef just south of Seal Cay, then headed southeast to Nicholas Cay in the Sapodillas. Our friends were there along with five other sailboats. It was a beautiful spot that had it all: clear turquoise water, palm trees, white sand beach and a nearby reef for fishing. It was everything we missed while we were up the Rio Dulce in Guatemala.

Ken managed to rally long enough to come on deck to set the anchor, then he went back to bed. He hurt all over along with the sweats and chills. I pulled out our medical book to look up Malaria. On the opposite page was Dengue Fever, also known as "Break Bone Fever". The description was exactly what Ken had experienced so far. I read down the list of symptoms and Ken had each one. He felt like every bone in his body was broken. He was miserable and the feeling just seemed to go on and on. Ibuprofen helped ease the pain only slightly. Aside from lots of liquids there wasn't much else I could do for him. There is no medicine for Dengue Fever. The high fever was frightening. One night when his temperature rose to 103 degrees, Ken mumbled, "I'm not going to school today." I told him it was OK, and he could stay home until he felt better. He never even remembered that conversation.

We learned that a specific kind of mosquito that bites during the day was the culprit for spreading this illness. It takes 7 -10 days to get sick so it was an unwanted parting souvenir from Guatemala! We had been so careful to use bug repellent. We always closed the boats screens and even burned mosquito coils to keep them out of the boat.

After four days Ken's fever broke and he started to feel better for several hours. Wham! All the symptoms were back again, with a red rash added, just as described in our medical book. It was at least eight days before the fever was completely gone but the aches and pains and weakness lasted several more weeks. We were fortunate to have friends nearby on the other boats that provided ice, Gatorade, fresh fish and sympathy during the ordeal. In the mornings I took a break from my nursing duties to walk on the island with my women friends from the other boats. At one end of the island was an unfinished resort owned by a Swiss man who was back in Switzerland. A caretaker lived there with his wife and three small children. After our walk we would do yoga or tai chi in an unfinished cabana at the building site. It was an inspiring location with a gentle breeze rustling the palms, chattering birds and water lapping at the shore. In fact, it was almost like those morning exercise shows on TV where the fitness fanatics are on an idyllic beach in Waikiki doing a seemingly effortless workout. But there were no perfect bodies and no spandex in our little group—just some fun, middle-aged women trying to keep fit.

Thanksgiving seemed to creep up on me. I was so preoccupied with Ken being sick that I hadn't even thought about Thanksgiving, much less planned any special food. Suddenly, it was the day before the holiday and one of my walking pals got on the VHF radio to coordinate a Thanksgiving feast on shore. They got permission from the caretaker to use the unfinished restaurant at the "resort" and invited his family to join the festivities. So on the radio that Wednesday morning Kim, our "party coordinator" said she was cooking a turkey breast, rosemary and garlic mashed potatoes, baking a coconut pie and home make rolls in the shape of teddy bears for the kids! *Impressive!* The next energetic woman said she was bringing turkey, cranberry sauce, two pumpkin pies, yams and rice. *Were these women for real??* The third cruising Martha Stewart offered to bring smoked Nova Scotia Salmon with capers and crackers, stuffing, corn and cherry cheesecake! *No way!*

Meanwhile, I listened in amazement as my turn approached. I wasn't prepared! I didn't think to buy a turkey two weeks ago in Guatemala. *What could I possibly add to that gourmet array? What would I do to save face?*

And there it was over the radio, "Jane, have you thought about it?"

Oh dear! I had to think fast and buy myself some time. I keyed the radio mike and stammered, "Uh...um.... I'll have to rummage through our provisions and see what I can come up with. I'll get back to you later."

I found one onion and one carrot and plenty of canned goods. But the last thing I wanted to do was turn on the oven and heat up the boat more while Ken was already sweating with fever. I managed to put together a pasta salad and another concoction from canned goods. I took my last bottle of wine to share, a can of black olives and some balloons and ribbons for decorations. It was a wonderful party complete with guitar and flute music that continued until dark. Poor Ken stayed in bed and slept through the whole affair, not wanting to move. I took him a big plate of food, which he enjoyed, later on the boat.

During the months of November and December one cold front after another comes down to the Northwest Caribbean from the United States. These cold fronts bring strong winds and squalls. Wherever we went we had to take that into consideration to find anchorages that were protected in all wind directions.

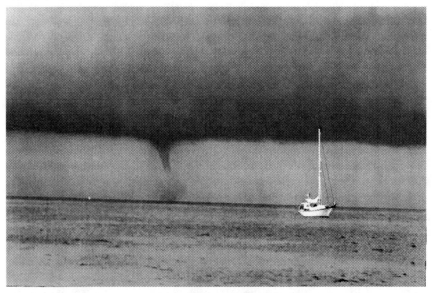

Waterspout in Belize

Once Ken felt better we sailed further up the coast on the mainland of Belize to the town of Placencia to replenish our supplies. Placencia is a quiet little village with houses built on stilts. Everyone goes barefoot. There is one sidewalk that serves as the main street. It's one mile long and took 30 years to complete.

For two weeks we zigzagged our way north moving from reef islands to mainland lagoons and back out to the islands. We stopped at Sapodilla Lagoon and anchored in perfect protection during a nasty front. It seemed like we were in a mountain lake. During our two days in Sapodilla Lagoon we worked hard to try to catch a Snook on a hand-line from the dinghy. The place looked so darn fishy. We had a couple big strikes and lost a lure. No Snook but we ended up with a nice barracuda and pompano for dinner.

We sailed out to Belize's Fly Range (a cluster of islands) and the Bluefield Range where we spotted a slow lumbering manatee near the mangroves. We sailed past Gallow Point and into the Drowned Cayes where several dolphins lingered lazily around us. Then we continued on through the shallow Port Stucko where we managed not to get stuck. It was a little stressful, however, since the average water depth was only 5 to 6 feet. There were stakes and branches sticking up out of the water all around us. Usually stakes or branches are used to mark shallow areas. We kept trying to avoid going aground by keeping all the stakes to starboard…until we figured out that they marked fish and lobster traps not shoals! Once that dawned on us the going got much easier.

When we were anchored at Cay Caulker a strange, intermittent screeching noise woke me before dawn. Puzzled, I eventually realized that the sound was close by but off the boat. I poked my head up out of our overhead hatch for a look around. The full moon was still out casting a soft, silvery-blue hue over the anchorage. Next to us, a local fisherman was hoisting the mainsail of his gaff-rigged sloop. Heave and screech, heave and screech. The boom extended out beyond the stern of the sleek narrow craft. There was no motor so the sail went up before he raised the anchor. Then out came the jib as he fell off to catch the gentle breeze. Ghosting over the glittering water the classic sailing workboat glided silently out of the harbor by the light of the moon. To me it was a most beautiful sight. To the fisherman it was another day off to work in search of fish.

December 12, 2000

From Cay Caulker our last stop in Belize was San Pedro on Ambergris Cay. San Pedro is a cute, cute town. The people there were hard at work to rebuild and repair after Hurricane Keith blasted it in October 2000. New roofs were being thatched and new coats of bright paint freshened things up for Christmas and the tourist season.

I don't know what the place looked like before the destruction but we still found it completely charming. Golf carts were the way to get around on the sand streets. There were plenty of little beachfront restaurants and Tiki bars. Christmas lights were strung along Barrier Reef Drive and the town square.

We even saw Santa Claus arrive at the elementary school in a golf cart. Ken's beard was quite bushy at the time. He was in the holiday spirit and would give a hearty "HO! HO! HO!" when he walked past little kids in town. They stared at him trying to figure out if this could really be St. Nick in shorts and T-shirt! Ken would ask them if they'd been good and give them a wink. Still unsure, but not taking any chances, the youngsters would nod their heads with a glimmer of hope in their eyes.

Back to back cold fronts kept us anchored in San Pedro for two weeks. On Christmas Eve, a rainsquall let up and allowed us to go ashore for a nice dinner at an open-air Italian restaurant on the beach under little twinkling white lights. Afterwards we strolled through town.

Families and friends gathered near the town square waiting for the midnight Christmas Eve service at the Catholic Church. Little girls were dressed up in frilly dresses and shiny buckled shoes. Boys with their shirttails askew ran around full of energy and probably wondered if tomorrow would ever come. We missed our own families, kids and grandchildren and wished we were with them all. Two days later we had a break in the weather and set off for Mexico.

Chapter 22
The Yucatan Peninsula

December 27, 2000

Breaking waves thundered on either side of our boat as we came to the buoy, made a dogleg turn to port and proceeded out the narrow cut in the reef to deep water. *Iniki* bravely surged ahead out the pass against the forceful incoming rush of the sea that funneled into the harbor of San Pedro, Belize. Ken and I were leaving Ambergris Cay, the northern most island of Belize. Once outside the reef we turned toward the neighboring country to the north—Mexico. We were soon cruising along the coast of the Yucatan Peninsula. Our ultimate goal was Isla Mujeres about 240 nautical miles away. But we had lots of places to stop along the way if need be.

We sailed all night with moderate winds. By the time morning came around the breezes were brisk. The clouds turned dark and foreboding. It began to drizzle. Who wants to be sailing in that stuff if you don't have to? We ducked into Bahia Espiritu Santo (Bay of the Holy Ghost) to wait for the squalls to pass. The next morning we set out again. It was very blustery and we were soon beating into 20-25 knots that continued all day and night. The extra 2-knot push from the north setting current was some consolation. From time to time high-speed ferries raced by us. They were running back and forth from Cozumel to Playa del Carmen on the mainland. A cruise ship was just anchoring and preparing to disembark its passengers at this popular port of call. Ken and I had visited Playa del Carmen in the 1980's and there wasn't much there except a few small diving resorts. What a change! Now dubbed "The Mayan Riviera", the coastline from Tulum to Playa del Carmen is one long continuous strip of condos and hotels.

The weather report that day announced another cold front heading toward us so we anchored behind the shelter of Hut Point on the mainland about 10 nautical miles north of Playa del Carmen. There was a rare stretch of undeveloped beach and no other boats around. Even though stiff north winds kept us there for five days over the New Year-2001, we were comfortable in the flat waters behind the reef. In fact, it was such a nice place to be anchored I was very surprised that there were no other cruisers enjoying the spot with us.

I had lobster tails in the freezer that I saved for our private little New Year's Eve celebration (I planned ahead this time!). No crowds, no traffic or parking problems, no uncomfortable neckties or high-heeled shoes—simply a barefoot, steamed lobster and champagne dinner for two aboard a boat gently bobbing at anchor off a white-sand beach in Mexico. It was simply the best! We enjoyed a few fireworks from a distant resort to the south of us, but couldn't stay awake until midnight to see in the New Year.

Ken and I realized we were getting "up north" again when we had to start closing hatches at night and dig out long sleeve T-shirts to keep warm. On New Year's Day Ken wanted to go spear fishing. The water was also cooler in Mexico so I dug out a wetsuit to wear so I wouldn't whine about being cold while we were snorkeling. We only saw one small lobster and a few small fish; nothing suitable for dinner. The current was quite strong so we got tired faster than normal but at least I stayed warm. Swimming back to our dinghy Ken was still hoping to find a grouper. He stuck his head under a coral ledge and came face to face with a six-foot nurse shark. Nurse sharks are not a problem if left unprovoked but I did not turn my back on it as we retreated. Once we were safely back in our dinghy Ken told me he actually thought for a moment about spearing that shark since shark meat is good to eat. The thought of a large angry shark thrashing about quickly changed his mind. Thank goodness common sense overruled the macho hunter!

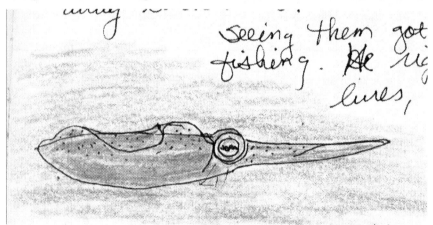

We made the trip from Hut Point to Isla Mujeres in one long day. We sailed along the seemingly endless, picture perfect, white sand beach of Cancun crowded with grand resorts all competing for the masses of pale tourists who flock to Mexico's premier playground for fun in the sun. A giant parasail displaying the big bat symbol of Baccardi Rum passed close enough to our boat for me to see the grinning face of the happy thrill-seeker waving to us. A small plane pulling a large advertising banner over the beachfront announced a 2 for 1 Happy Hour at Dady O's Bar. When we got a mile or so off the tip of Cancun's hotel zone the winds suddenly piped up and got very fluky. The crazy currents slowed our progress. Going into the wind I had an odd sensation that we were really flying but making no headway at all. I was at the helm concentrating to keep us on course while Ken studied the charts for our approach to Isla Mujeres (Island of Women) that was 7 nautical miles northeast of Cancun. We had been trolling all day but caught nothing except floating weeds. Naturally, just then, when we were both preoccupied with a situation that required our attention, a fish hit our lure and took off on a run. Ken had fun reeling in the barracuda and proceeded to clean it in the cockpit as we slam-banged on toward Isla Mujeres. That last 7 miles of the day seemed like 20 to me. Finally we arrived at the northwest end of Isla Mujeres and followed the marked channel into the bay. We anchored in time to sit down to watch the sunset and spot all the boats we knew in the harbor.

It had been twelve days since we last saw a town. I was anxious to get off the boat and look around. I was sure there was a jumbo margarita calling to me from an authentic little Mexican taco joint! But we were so tired I settled for a cold beer and fresh fish on board that night---not too shabby. The margarita and tacos could wait.

The next day was a local holiday--Three Kings Day. Another cruiser warned us that if we checked in that day we would be charged overtime instead of the normal fees. We had already been in Mexican waters for two weeks without checking in with Customs and Immigration due to our remote stops along the way up from Belize. So we chose to go ashore and check in ASAP.

When we got to the Port Captain's office with our stamped paperwork there were two rather loud American men ahead of us who had arrived from Florida. They made no attempt to speak Spanish—not even 'hello'. They showed no respect for this official in his white pressed navy uniform. The officer was still polite, took their papers and explained the overtime charge. The two men paid and left. Ken and I were next, aware of the lack of courtesy the previous pair showed. Respect and politeness were important when dealing with foreign government officials. We also learned in our Latin American travels that it rude to walk into a room and just start talking without first greeting whoever is present. (A polite thing to do anywhere, for that matter) Even a meager attempt at the local language and a show of interest in the town and culture is always appreciated. Plus, we have gotten a lot of helpful local information this way...for example, who makes the best tacos and margaritas on the island?

We had a friendly conversation with the Port Captain in a mixture of Spanish and English. We were charged the normal fees with no mention of overtime charges. *Hmmm. Interesting!*

Ken and I found Isla Mujeres very charming. I couldn't really name anything specific that made it unique. It was just a comfortable feeling--a real Mexican community (as opposed to the hotel strip in Cancun). It was quiet, peaceful, safe and we felt welcome. Coming to Mexico seemed like a big step up in the world for us. From Isla Mujeres we could take a fast ferry and be in Cancun in eighteen minutes. Once in Cancun one could find just about anything. There was a Sam's Club, Walmart, first class shopping malls, movie theaters and all the fast food chains. *Funny how the status and desire for fast food is elevated when you are denied it for a long time!* There was enough action in Cancun to mix with the laid-back beach time in Isla Mujeres to make it a fun place for our daughters, Kassie and Tina, son-in-law Jaime and granddaughter Daisy to come visit us in January for 10 days.

Since it was a mega tourist area many of the restaurants made an attempt to be helpful by translating their menu into English. Sometimes that proved to be a great source of amusement for me. Grilled fish became: "fish to the natural one on the grill". Fried fish was: "fillet of having fished breaded". Sautéed squid was really elevated to: "Squid to the pleasure". It all added to the colorful tropical dining atmosphere!

February 2001

We put *Iniki* into Marina Paraiso on Isla Mujeres so we could travel inland in the Yucatan Peninsula. From Cancun we boarded a bus and rode four hours on a super highway through scrub brush to the city of Merida. Even though it was a deluxe bus, Ken's back was killing him long before we reached our destination. He declared that he was not returning on that bus! We arrived in the colonial city of Merida on Friday, the first day of Carnival. Five days of parades were scheduled from Friday to Tuesday before Ash Wednesday. The whole weekend was very civil and calm--no drunks and no fights--just families out enjoying the festivities and eating. Vendors lined the parade route. They sold tacos al pastor, tamales, churros, corn on the cob, fresh fruit, and big pieces of fried pigskin.

Supposedly, each parade had a different theme. However, the three that we watched were identical and by Monday morning we'd had enough of the crowds. We rented a car and drove south out of Merida following the Puuc Route, which means hill route. The map showed that it would lead us to several sites of Mayan ruins and cenotes (underground wells). We managed to find our way to Uxmal (oosh-mal) by late afternoon, an accomplishment in itself due to the lack of road signs. At Uxmal we were pleasantly surprised to find a lovely lodge directly across the road from the entrance to the site. At sundown that same evening we went into the park for the laser light show amid the ruins. We climbed to the top of one of the buildings on the plaza. Bats emerged from the vacant temples to swoop overhead with the nighthawks as the moon and stars appeared. The mood created was eerie and ghostly. *Can the light show possibly top this?* As soon as it was dark the music began. The relief designs on the different structures were illuminated as the narrator told a story of the ancient people who once thrived there. The Puuc style has far more artistic decoration and animal imagery on the buildings in this part of Mexico than the larger temples of Tikal in Guatemala.

We returned to the park the next morning as soon as it opened, following some good advice for viewing the ruins. That advice was to go early in the morning before it gets too hot and before all the crowds arrive in the big tour buses. We were through and left the park just as the buses began to roll in. Thank goodness our rental car was new and our air conditioning worked! The searing heat of the day rose off the pavement creating dancing mirages. Stops for directions were required a few times as we drove through one small town after another: Ticul, Mama, Chumayel, Teabo, Sotuta, Holca, Piste and finally we arrived at the well-known Mayan site, Chichen Itza.

We employed the same touring strategy at Chichen Itza and entered when the gates opened at 8:00AM. Three hours was plenty for us. We had reached saturation level in our education of Mayan ruins! We were gone before the crowds and the Yucatan sun became unbearable. By sundown we were back in Cancun and Isla Mujeres.

Chapter 23
Mexico to Florida

April 24, 2001

The Yucatan Channel runs between the Yucatan Peninsula of Mexico and the island of Cuba allowing the waters of the Caribbean Sea to flow into the Gulf of Mexico and the Straits of Florida. This creates the strong current known as the Gulf Stream.

There are numerous offshoots from the Gulf Stream that loop around, turn back, and create swirling eddies that play havoc with sailors underway. Add heavy shipping traffic to the equation and the challenges of the passage between Mexico and Florida become more apparent.

Ken and I had been aboard *Iniki* in Isla Mujeres, Mexico (near Cancun) for four months. The frontal weather systems that march down from the northwest during the winter months usually ease up by spring. This year they continued into April and May keeping us waiting for favorable sailing conditions to go north. It is approximately a 350 nautical mile passage so the average sailboat needs a three to four day weather window. Many cruisers around us in the harbor got antsy to go and acquired an attitude of, "That's it! We're leaving tomorrow. The forecast doesn't sound too bad." Others ignore the forecast and say, "It's a piece of cake. Just get in the Gulf Stream and ride the current up to Florida!"

I was excited about getting *Iniki* back in U.S. waters again but I'd be lying if I said I was looking forward to the passage. While we waited for safe and comfortable conditions we heard horror stories from failed attempts by impatient sailors. Two boats were dismasted five miles out and limped back to Isla Mujeres. Others tried to leave up to four or five times only to turn back because of rough unpleasant rides. We waited some more.

On Wednesday May 2, 2001 Ken and I said "Adios!" to Mexico. A fleet of sport fishing boats raced past us at top speed to get out to the fishing grounds ten to fifteen miles out. It took us three hours to catch up to them. Sailfish were leaping completely out of the water all over the place. It was quite exciting to see. I counted thirty tuna-towered fishing boats out there in pursuit of the prize catch.

We had 10 knots of wind all day with two to three foot swells—quite nice. By evening the winds were 18-20 knots on the nose. On my 9:00 PM-midnight shift the autopilot kept beeping a warning that we were off course. I looked things over with a flashlight and saw that a couple of screws had come out and the plastic bracket that held it in place cracked and was falling apart. I woke up Ken. He reattached the mechanism but the autopilot wouldn't work which meant hand steering the rest of the trip. In the morning the winds shifted more against us and we were slowed down by counter currents. We decided to change course and head for the coast of Cuba. We were near the western most point of the island called Cabo San Antonio. By 1:30 Thursday afternoon, we passed through the wide break in the reef. Immediately, some sea monster attacked our fishing lure with a vengeance and took off. Ken donned the fighting belt and it took all his strength to just hang on to the pole. The line was just flying out. I literally had to pour some water on the reel to cool it down. After a forty-minute fight the line snapped and the creature was gone.

We motored a couple more hours into the Golfo de Guanahacabibes and anchored in the lagoon of Los Cayos de la Lena. It's a very remote corner of Cuba—no towns and nowhere to even go ashore. Likewise, there was no place to check in and no patrolling officials. Ken decided no one lives there because they can't pronounce "Guanahacabibes"!

From there we could move along the coast behind the reef in protected water for nearly 100 miles. The farther east we could get along the coast the better the angle on the wind to cross over to the Dry Tortugas or Key West.

Two other sailboats arrived the next day and anchored near us. We had heard them on the VHF radio during our crossing from Mexico and knew that they left Isla Mujeres the same day we did. But when we stopped they continued on for another extra 24 hours, making very little headway against the winds and currents. They gave up, turned around and entered the lagoon to rest and wait for better conditions.

The slow moving low-pressure system stalled over us for days causing strong NE winds and 7-8 ft. seas. At least we were in a snug, well-protected place to wait it out with plenty of fish to catch in the maze of mangroves. We had a blast catching our dinner on a handline. I even hooked about a 50 lb. tarpon! It did one of those magnificent tail walks they are famous for. Then as we watched, mouths agape, it shook its head, spit out the lure and landed with a grand splash.

Two more sailboats arrived. While we all waited for the low to dissipate we got to know each other, traded books and movies and told tales of our travels. We were there nine days before we all moved on. Two went south, and two went offshore toward Florida. Ken and I made our way north up the coast, tacking inside the reef. We hadn't done so much tacking in ages. I was exhausted after a day of hauling, grinding and reefing. We caught no fish that day but a stupid tern picked up our fishing lure five times and tried to fly off with it.

Cuban fisherman on inner tubes lashed together

On Day 11 in Cuba we caught up with a group of boats that left Mexico three days before we did. We witnessed, once again, how willing cruisers are to help each other out. I thought we would be in Florida three days after we left Mexico so I shopped for food accordingly. Now, all the boaters were running out of things and trading this and that. We got a few extra gallons of fuel we needed and gave out water, toilet paper, fishing lures and reading books. Ken was also thrilled to trade for some popcorn!

Two Austrian flagged catamarans arrived in that bay later in the day. One of the men rowed over to our boat and handed us some papers. We had never met him before. Apparently, when we checked out of Mexico, our Mexican import papers for Iniki didn't get returned to us with our Zarpe (exit papers). Instead, the papers somehow got attached by mistake to the exit papers of a German sailboat. The German boat gave our papers to the Austrian boat headed for Cuba in case they caught up to us. A lot of details were unclear since this Austrian did not speak a lot of English. Since we did not plan to stop in Cuba, they must have heard us on the radio. I was just amazed at all the effort made by several people we didn't even know to get those papers to us!

After two weeks along the northwest Coast of Cuba we had a good weather window to sail home. From Punta Alonso Rojos we motored north inside the reef for five miles to the Galera cut and out into deep water. It was a wonderful sail in calm seas and 10 knots of ENE winds. We were going a bit slow, though with currents against us. *Where IS that Gulf Stream?* I, for one, was not complaining one bit. I'll take slow and easy any day.

The Navigator reading the chart and water

I was really enjoying the passage. Dolphins danced at our bow. Flying fish defied gravity as they soared great distances above the surface. Just when I was sure they could go no further, they would continue on 10 more yards before dropping back into the water.

I was at the helm that afternoon while Ken napped. With the winds being so light, I had the autopilot (which Ken fixed) off so I could hand steer closer to the wind. I left the wheel for a second to check our position and speed on the GPS. The jib back winded and we were unintentionally hoved to and stopped. *No problem…. Ken wanted to run the engine a while anyway to pick up some speed.* I started the engine, forgetting that we had a fishing line out. When I put the boat in gear and turned, I heard a "snap". I knew instantly what had happened. I had just fouled the line around the propeller! *(#@!#!)* I quickly shifted to neutral as I cursed my stupidity. I hated to have to tell Ken what I had done. But Ken loves these little challenges and quickly shifted into problem solving mode. We killed the engine and dropped the sails. I retrieved Ken's mask and fins while he threw the life sling out into the water as a safety precaution. A horrifying thought entered my mind. *What if he gets into the water and is carried away by the current while I'm on board alone with an engine crippled by a fouled prop?* I pushed that thought away by thinking about all the factors in our favor: 1) It was daylight. 2) There was virtually no wind and very little current. 3) The sea was flat calm.

Ken didn't drift away. He easily cut the fishing line off the propeller and enjoyed the little swim in the clear, warm, indigo water. We were soon underway again with yet another lure offered to Davey Jones's Locker!

We found the Gulf Stream at dusk and really started to make some way. The planet Mars rose bright and red in the eastern night sky. We did not see one ship all night. It was the most pleasant overnight sail I can remember. By 10:00am the next morning the lighthouse of the Dry Tortugas was in sight. The American flag proudly waved atop the flagpole at Fort Jefferson. I am always surprised at the depth of emotion and pride that symbol of freedom stirs up in me when I return home after traveling out of the country.

We toured the fort, stayed overnight and then sailed east 40 miles to the Marqueses Keys for the following night. I couldn't wait to get to Key West the next day. It had been a long time since we had been in any sort of town. I looked forward to having pizza, cold beer, ice cream, a laundromat and telephones!

Chapter 24
Salute to Life

May 19, 2001

Jimmy Buffet tunes blared from our stereo as we sailed up the Key West Channel and completed our circle of the Caribbean. The last time we sailed that channel was in January 1997. *Iniki* glided by the waterfront and Mallory Square, just one more sailboat hardly noticed among the large fleet there. But I was getting emotional again, thinking about our whole adventure that Ken and I had done together. I was so proud of Ken, for making it happen, for being such a knowledgeable and skillful Captain/Weatherman, and for keeping us safe through all kinds of situations over the past five years aboard *Iniki*. I was proud of myself, as well. I was able to overcome my apprehensions and make the drastic lifestyle changes in order to go —only to discover an open door to wonderful life experiences that would never have been possible otherwise. It was a complete change in direction for me. Sailing off into the sunset gave me time to come into myself again. It was a slow process that I don't think I was even aware of at first. It was a gradual transformation nurtured and nourished by slow days and open spaces; by being immersed in Nature, learning the rhythm of her heartbeat, reflecting on flaming sunsets and immense starry night skies out at sea. The places we saw, the people we met, the cultures we experienced and the sense of self-sufficiency we acquired forever altered our perspective of life and developed a core of inner strength within us both. The journey for me was a life lesson in dealing with the unexpected challenges that confront us throughout a lifetime. The more experiences I accumulate the more tools and resources I have to draw from to handle the challenges as they come. This stretching and personal growth has led me to new levels of self-confidence and cultivated the mental toughness that I needed to endure my cancer treatments and move on with my life. I will continue to process these changes and integrate them into my life no matter what direction the wind blows. The revelations of my journey reveal themselves like surprise gifts, coming unexpectedly in moments of quiet reflection.

So on the pier that evening in Key West, bathed in the glow of an appropriately flamboyant setting sun, my soul mate and I clinked our glasses to the completion of our Caribbean sojourn and began to plan our next adventure-- "Salute", to life!

Iniki

Epilogue

Ken and Jane sold *Iniki* and moved aboard *Salute*, a fifty foot Grand Banks trawler. They settled in Stuart, Florida for the next three years at the Hutchinson Island Marriott Marina as they transitioned back to "landlubber' society. *Salute* provided more space and comfort that Jane was ready for. At the same time Ken could remain on the water. It was a good compromise.

Salute in Stuart, Florida

Jane got her Florida Real Estate license and began a new career while Ken resumed his practice as a Clinical Hypnotherapist.

In April, 2004 they sold *Salute* and moved to Sacramento, California to be near their kids and grandchildren. Timing is everything. Just after they left, four hurricanes slammed Florida with devastating results. Ivan and Jeanne were direct hits on Hutchinson Island and Stuart.

Jane continues to live an adventurous and cancer-free life. She welcomes any questions about live-aboard cruising or surviving breast cancer. Her email address is: Jane@JaneGrossman.com. For information on self-hypnosis programs and CDs, please visit www.KenGrossman.com.

About the Author

Jane Grossman learned to sail on Lake Michigan just three years before sailing away to the Caribbean. She and her husband, Ken spent the next 8 years as full time "liveaboards". Jane wrote articles for "The Binnacle", Columbia Yacht Club's monthly newsletter during their travels so others could follow their adventure.

She and Ken currently reside on solid ground in Sacramento, California. (Ken is boat shopping again.)

Jane's email is <u>Jane@JaneGrossman.com</u> .

"If one woman finds inspiration from these pages and the courage to face her own challenges then my goal has been accomplished."

- Jane Grossman

Printed in the United States
109275LV00007B/235-237/A

9 781420 837599